GLOUCESTERSHIRE COUNTY LIBRARIES.

CP

THE SECRET TENT

A Play in Three Acts

by

ELIZABETH ADDYMAN

ENGLISH THEATRE GUILD LTD.
ASCOT HOUSE, 52 DEAN STREET, LONDON, W.1

PRINTED IN GREAT BRITAIN BY THE WHITEFRIARS PRESS LTD.
LONDON AND TONBRIDGE

PRESS APPRECIATIONS

" After two fearsome evenings spent in West End theatres lately with plays intended for runs, it was a refreshing change last night for me to go to the Strand, and see the Repertory Players try out a piece which had vigour and interest. This was ' The Secret Tent,' by Elizabeth Addyman. . . . Every single one of the cast has an actable part, and plays it with skill." —W. A. DARLINGTON in the *Daily Telegraph.*

" It has some of the most tantalizing curtains ever invented, leaving the audience aching for the intervals to end."—*Daily Express.*

" This highly dramatic and moving play . . . is a triumph for all concerned, and an auspicious beginning as an author for Elizabeth Addyman. She has made a surprisingly good job of her first play which, embellished by impeccable acting, grips the audience, and stirs the emotions. . . . ' The Secret Tent ' definitely has a lot to recommend it."—*The Northern Daily Telegraph.*

" I had, at the Theatre Royal last night, an experience such as I have not had since I witnessed the first performance of Emlyn Williams in ' Night Must Fall.' I went, all unsuspecting, to a play which caught me at the throat, kicked me in the stomach, and left me limp at the knees. That's ' The Secret Tent ' by Elizabeth Addyman. I defy the world's most cynical theatre-goer to see the end of the second act and not wait to see what happens in the third. I wouldn't dream of revealing the plot to you, but it has a murder, and a disappearance, and a true romance, and characters who behave as human beings really do behave, and not as people in a play." —*Glasgow Evening News.*

" This first play by Elizabeth Addyman builds tension through two acts and has the customers gasping in the third. Play, capably acted, is one of the best seen at this legit house for months."—*Variety*, New York.

" The play had its first public presentation at the Grand Theatre, Blackpool, last night when it merited its immediate enthusiastic success."— *News Chronicle.*

First performed by the Repertory Players at the Strand Theatre, London, on Sunday, October 4th, 1953.

CHRISTOPHER MARTYN	*Gordon Whiting*
RUTH MARTYN	*Mary Mackenzie*
NAOMI MARTYN	*Mary Merrall*
MISS MITCHUM-BROWNE	*Barbara Leake*
ERNIE BRIGGS	*Robert Desmond*
INSPECTOR THORNTON	*Ewan Roberts*
MISS PEARCE	*Gwynne Whitby*

Produced by JOAN SWINSTEAD.

And subsequently presented by George and Alfred Black Ltd., with the following cast :—

CHRISTOPHER MARTYN	*Richard Greene*
RUTH MARTYN	*Mary Mackenzie*
NAOMI MARTYN	*Nora Swinburne*
MISS MITCHUM-BROWNE	*Patience Collier*
ERNIE BRIGGS	*Robert Desmond*
INSPECTOR THORNTON	*Ewan Roberts*
MISS PEARCE	*Gwynne Whitby*

Produced by JOAN SWINSTEAD.

CHARACTERS

(in order of appearance)

CHRISTOPHER MARTYN.
RUTH MARTYN, *his wife.*
NAOMI MARTYN, *his mother.*
MISS MITCHUM-BROWNE.
ERNIE BRIGGS.
INSPECTOR THORNTON.
MISS PEARCE.

The whole action of the play takes place in the living room of an old cottage in East Kent, during four days in October.

ACT I, SCENE 1 : *Thursday evening.*
        SCENE 2 : *Friday evening.*
ACT II :   *Saturday morning.*
ACT III :   *Sunday afternoon.*

THE SECRET TENT

ACT I

Scene 1. (*Thursday*)

The living room of Oak Cottage. It is old and beamed, and belongs to people who run a chicken farm, signs of which are about the place. In the back wall is the front door, slightly L.C. *To the* L. *of it is a long casement window, with window-seat. Up* R. *is a small staircase, leading to the upper regions. Down* R. *is a door leading to the kitchen. In the* L. *wall is an open fireplace. Between the staircase and the front door is a dresser, on which is the telephone. An arm chair is above the fireplace. To* R.C. *a table with three chairs round it. (See Plan.)*

It is six o'clock on an autumn evening. The room is in great disorder—toys scattered all over the place, and the remains of a baby's toilet in front of the fire—bath, basket, clothes-horse with nappies, etc. CHRISTOPHER MARTYN *is sitting at the table, which is littered with materials from which he has been making a model ship, and to which he is hurriedly putting the finishing touches. He wears an old dressing gown over evening dress shirt and trousers. Sounds of a small boy being put to bed come from upstairs.*

RUTH (*appearing at the top of the stairs*). Now stop it, Peter darling—there's a good boy—or you'll wake Ba.

PETER (*off*). But I want my ship!

RUTH. Well Daddy'll bring it in a minute. (*She comes downstairs, carrying a new red mackintosh over her arm.*) Oh Chris, haven't you finished that yet?

CHRIS (*engrossed*). Practically.

RUTH. You're running things awfully late.

CHRIS. I'm dressed all but my coat—and it's got a button off. Could you fix it for me?

RUTH (*flinging the mackintosh over the back of a chair, and hunting for her work box in the muddle*). Did you make sure about that bottom pen?

CHRIS. Oh lord—I forgot!

RUTH. Never mind, I'll have time to see to it before **I go.** Where's your coat?

CHRIS. Um ?

RUTH. Your coat !

CHRIS. Oh—on the back of that chair. (*He looks up, and sees the mackintosh, which is over his dinner jacket.*) What's that flashy looking object, may I ask ?

RUTH (*putting work box on table and picking up the mac.*). My new Paris model ! Like it ? (*She holds it up for him to see.*)

CHRIS. Most dashing. (*He returns to the ship. Ruth puts mac. down, sits opposite him at table, and begins to sew on button.*) How much did you rush me for that ?

RUTH. Guess ?

CHRIS. Far more than I can afford when I haven't paid for those new pullets yet !

RUTH. It wasn't—honest ! 39/11 at Marks and Spencers ! I couldn't resist it—d'you mind ?

CHRIS. Of course I don't mind—bless you ! Not that you need any new clothes—you always look nice, whatever you wear.

RUTH. A typically husbandly remark ! Gosh—this dinner jacket's an object—but of course *you* always look nice whatever you wear too !

CHRIS. Idiot ! I've inked in the worst moth holes.

RUTH. Does it still fit ?

CHRIS. Just. (*Leaning back, looking at his model.*) Does that rigging look right to you ?

RUTH. Darling, what's the good of asking me ? You ought to know. You were in the Navy.

CHRIS. My sweet—I was in the Battle of the Atlantic—not the Battle of the Nile ! (*He looks at the button she is sewing on.*) That doesn't match !

RUTH. Near enough—it's the best I can do, anyway. (*She bites off cotton.*) Come on, ducky—buck up ! I simply must do something about this room before Naomi gets here.

CHRIS (*cheerfully*). Oh she won't notice.

RUTH. Won't she just ! (*She puts coat over back of chair, leaving work basket on table, and begins to clear up the baby's things. There are sounds of Peter pattering overhead.*) Oh dear, he's out of bed again ! He is a little pest on Thursday nights.

CHRIS. I'll take this up to him in a minute—that'll settle him.

RUTH (*going to top of stairs*). If he bangs about like that he'll wake Ba—and then I'll never get off. Peter ! Get back to bed ! (*She disappears for a minute, and has an argument with Peter in the distance.*)

(CHRIS *has finished the ship. He wipes his hands, picks up his evening jacket, and backs away from the ship having a final look at it while he puts on coat.* RUTH *returns, and continues clearing up while she talks.*)

RUTH. She's never batted an eyelid, bless her. She's a much better baby than Peter was.

CHRIS (*at fireplace, straightening himself up*). Possibly because her Mummie was a much calmer woman before she was born.

RUTH. Yes—I suppose I was. I—I felt much better—that was why.

CHRIS. Funny—because you weren't so well!

RUTH. I mean better inside!

CHRIS. You and your inside!

RUTH. That dinner jacket looks tighter than ever. You've put on weight since last year.

CHRIS. That's your fault—you shouldn't feed me so well!

RUTH. Nonsense! It's all the beer you drink. Oh, that reminds me—is there any left? It's Ernie's morning to-morrow.

CHRIS. Yes, there's a bottle been opened. Give him that. He won't notice if it's a bit flat.

RUTH. Stingy beast!

CHRIS. Oh dear—I wish I wasn't going to-night.

RUTH. You say that every year—but you always come back hilariously happy, I notice.

CHRIS. I'm getting too ancient for Old Boys' dinners. There are too many faces missing now—and the rest seem such kids. I'd much sooner be doing our usual Thursday pub crawl and flick. (*He hugs her.*) It's indecent to be so much in love with your wife after five years!

RUTH. Five and a half. (*Pushing him away.*) Now off you go, or you'll have to rush. I hope Minnie'll get you there all right.

CHRIS. Don't worry. She's running beautifully since she was decarbonized.

RUTH. Darling, promise me you'll go easy on the drink. I'm never happy 'till you get home after these do's.

CHRIS. Woman, are you suggesting that I ever return from " These do's," as you call them, in an inebriated condition?

RUTH. No, dear! But you *did* wake me up last time to tell me a long story about Nanny White who'd apparently been in the Lower Fourth with you!

CHRIS. I don't remember even mentioning Nanny White!

RUTH. I didn't expect you would !

CHRIS. Alright! Alright! I shall drink nothing but barley water, and drive home in second gear. So stop conjuring up visions of my mangled remains strewn across the road.

RUTH (*stopping in her tracks*). Don't talk like that, Chris. I couldn't live without you now.

CHRIS. Well, you won't have to. I'm your old man of the sea. I'll be clinging on to your shoulders when I'm eighty—then you'll be sorry you married someone old enough to be your father.

RUTH. You're not old enough to be my father !

CHRIS. I might if I'd been enterprising !

RUTH. At ten ?

CHRIS. Anyway, stop being macabre. What are you going to see to-night ?

RUTH. Haven't an earthly. Sally said to meet her outside the Odeon, and we'd chance what was on.

(*The banging overhead is coming into evidence again.*)

There's that little wretch again ! (*She starts for the stairs.*)

CHRIS. All right—leave that young man to me. (*At foot of stairs.*) Peter !

(*More scuttling and giggles.*)

PETER ! Get into bed at once.

PETER'S VOICE. Why ?

CHRIS. Because it's bed time—d'you want me to bring that ship up before I go ?

PETER'S VOICE. Yes.

CHRIS. Then get into bed before I count three. One—two

(*A hasty patter of small feet.*)

—three.

(CHRIS *looks pleased with himself, and straightens his tie as he moves back into the room.*)

That's settled him ! You only want to be firm with him.

RUTH. All right, all right, I know. One word from Father !

CHRIS. If you and Mother had sole charge of him he'd end up in Borstal.

RUTH (*with vehemence*). He *wouldn't.*

CHRIS (*teasing*). Probably will in any case. He's got spiv written all over him in block letters. Well! he doesn't get it from *my* side of the family.

RUTH. Shut up! Shut up!

CHRIS (*seeing she's serious*). Sorry, darling, I was only trying to be funny. Can't you bear aspersions on your ewe lamb? (*He puts his arm round her.*) We'll buy him a pair of specs and turn him into a Youth Leader, shall we?

RUTH (*still very serious*). We'll make them both happy—then they'll be good.

CHRIS (*looking down at her, his arm still round her*). So serious? What a funny kid you are! But I'm glad I married you, Mrs. Martyn! I must go. Give me a kiss.

(*Instead of the wifely salute he is expecting, she kisses him with passion. He is surprised.*)

Here, what's up?

RUTH. Just that I love you all three so terribly.

CHRIS. I'm quite fond of you all myself! Give me another— I like that, too!

(*They kiss again, ardently. Whilst they are embracing, NAOMI MARTYN opens the outer door, and walks in.*)

NAOMI. Good evening. Am I interrupting?

RUTH (*disengaging herself with some embarrassment*). Oh— hello, Naomi. . . .

NAOMI. Perhaps I should have knocked? He's smudged your lipstick, by the way.

RUTH. Has he? (*She goes to overmantel, and deals with her face.*)

NAOMI. Am I early? I thought you'd have gone, Chris.

CHRIS. I'm just off.

NAOMI. Well, you'd better remove the strawberry jam from your mouth before you go! (*She hands him a handkerchief from her bag.*)

RUTH (*quickly*). No—don't mess that up, Naomi. Here— have mine! (*She hands CHRIS hers.*)

NAOMI. Just as you like. (*She replaces her handkerchief in her bag. The atmosphere is a bit strained.*)

CHRIS (*having wiped his mouth—to RUTH*). Alright now?

RUTH. Let me. (*She polishes off his mouth.* NAOMI *regards them coldly.*)

NAOMI. It's quite a pleasant evening after the rain.

RUTH (*nervously*). Horrid afternoon, wasn't it? I never got the children outside. I'm afraid the room's in an awful mess.

NAOMI. Looks much as usual to me!

RUTH. You must blame Chris for the table—he always throws things around when he's concentrating!

NAOMI. Really? He always seemed remarkably tidy as a boy! What's that you're making, Chris?

CHRIS. A three-masted brig for Peter. Look alright to you?

NAOMI. Most impressive. Not that I'd know if it was right or not.

CHRIS. And you the daughter of an Admiral!

NAOMI. I never sailed before the mast with him! Shall I take it up to Peter?

CHRIS (*snatching it up*). Not on your life! It's taken me a whole week to make—nobody gives it to him but me!

NAOMI. Very well—but hadn't you better hurry up? Are you catching the 6.40 bus, Ruth?

RUTH. Yes. Sally's meeting me at seven.

CHRIS (*to his Mother*). And what devilment are *you* getting up to to-night?

NAOMI. I've brought my library book and my knitting. I'll be quite happy, so long as Miss Browne doesn't drop in.

CHRIS. Miss Mitchum-Browne, please! Well, if she does, you might persuade her to do something about that damp patch in the scullery.

NAOMI. Indeed I shan't! She's your landlady, not mine.

RUTH. Oh Chris we can't! She's so poor—I'm sure that she's nothing but our rent to live on. I always feel so sorry for her.

CHRIS (*as he goes, laughing*). For heaven's sake stop her, Mother! This is rapidly becoming a home from home for every-body Ruth feels sorry for—including the village idiot! Shan't be a tick. (*He disappears upstairs, where the ship is greeted rapturously by* PETER.)

RUTH (*indignantly*). Ernie is *not* the village idiot!

NAOMI. Quite a keen intellect, in fact! (*She looks at* RUTH's *overflowing workbasket on the table.*) Shall I get on with some of this mending for you while you're out?

RUTH (*gathering it together, and removing it hastily*). No—please don't bother. You won't have to cope with Miss Browne to-night

—there's a Bazaar Committee meeting up at Clifton Manor. She told me so when she collected the rent yesterday.

NAOMI. Good—then I can have a quiet read. Is Peter's cold better ?

RUTH. More or less. He's still a bit snuffly.

NAOMI. He seemed very lightly clad when I saw him out the other day. Hasn't he got anything warmer than those thin little overalls ?

RUTH. Oh I think he's alright. Kid's easily get over-heated when they're running about.

NAOMI. That's just the danger. However, I suppose you know best.

(Conversation flags.)

RUTH. I've—I've put your supper on a tray in the kitchen.

NAOMI. Thank you.

RUTH. You don't mind eggs, do you ?

NAOMI. I like them when they're new laid. Are the new pullets doing any good yet ?

RUTH. No—not really.

NAOMI. Did you try mixing ginger with the bran, as I suggested ?

RUTH. I don't know—I think Chris did. Oh that reminds me. I must just go and see if the bottom pen's secure. Ernie said something about a fox in Ford Spinney yesterday. Will you excuse me ?

NAOMI. You'd better hurry up, hadn't you ?

RUTH. It won't take me a minute.

(She goes through the outer door, glad to escape. NAOMI sighs gently. She starts clearly up the mess on the table, and picks up a sock that RUTH has dropped. There is a large hole in it. The noises from above come into evidence. She moves to foot of stairs.)

NAOMI *(calling)*. What *are* you doing, Christopher ? You're driving yourself frightfully late.

CHRIS *(coming downstairs. He is very dishevelled, with his tie undone, and his hair ruffled)*. The little devil ! Just look what he's done to me ! *(He goes to overmantel to put himself straight.)*

NAOMI *(continuing to tidy up)*. You and your son are about the same age. It's lucky I come here once a week to keep him in order. If he were left entirely to you and Ruth, I don't know where he'd end up !

CHRIS. Funny ! I seem to have had this conversation once before this evening ! (*Feeling in his pockets.*) Cigarettes ? Yes. Matches ? (*He looks along the mantelpiece.*)

NAOMI (*producing some from her bag*). Here you are.

CHRIS. Oh—thanks. (*He takes them from her.*) How are you getting back ?

NAOMI. Walking. I don't imagine you'll be in a fit condition to drive me home in that Heath Robinson contraption of yours !

CHRIS. To hear my womenfolk talk, you'd think I was in the last stages of D.Ts. And do be careful about Minnie—she's only just outside, and she's very touchy about her appearance.

NAOMI. I don't blame her—she looks as though she'd been a debutante in 1925 !

CHRIS. What a libel ! She's a perfectly good 1933 Baby Austin !

NAOMI (*looking up and listening*). There's an ominous silence. Does that mean Peter's asleep ?

CHRIS. Not on your life. I left him trying out his new ship in the bath !

NAOMI. Oh really, Chris ! I'd better go up at once.

CHRIS. Perhaps you had. Is it a frightful bore, baby sitting each week ?

NAOMI (*tartly*). Not at all—I appreciate being allowed a share of my grandchildren ! May I take a peep at Ba—or will it disturb her ?

CHRIS. Lord no—wild horses won't disturb her when she's asleep !

NAOMI. Thanks *very* much ! (*She goes upstairs—there is more chat as she removes Peter from the bathroom.*)

(CHRIS *looks at the clock on the mantelpiece, compares the time with his watch, mutters* " Good lord " *and gets a battered old hat and mackintosh from behind the outer door. He is just struggling in to the latter when* RUTH *comes in from outside. A completely changed* RUTH, *shaken as if she has seen a ghost—but* CHRIS *is too busy getting off to notice. He buttons up his mac. and shoves his hat on.*)

CHRIS. I must fly, darling. (*He kisses her.*) I'll probably be back about twelve—but don't worry if I'm later. (*He goes to foot of stairs and shouts*) 'Bye, Mother. See you next week.

(*He exits through outer door. There are sounds of Minnie in labour, and then, with a minor explosion, they disappear down the lane. Left alone, a desperate look comes over* RUTH'S *face. She looks out of the window, and comes back into the room, clasping her hand to her forehead. She goes to foot of stairs and listens—then moves to the dresser and gets her purse out of the drawer. She counts the money in it—there isn't enough. She goes to an ornament on the mantelpiece and empties out more money, which she puts in her purse. As she is doing so,* NAOMI *comes down stairs.*)

NAOMI. Can Peter have some milk ?

RUTH (*starting slightly, and turning*). What ? Oh yes—yes—I'll get it. (*She pushes past* NAOMI, *and goes out to the kitchen.*)

(NAOMI *lifts her eyebrows, and sighs again. She switches on the light, and goes over to the window to draw the curtains. Her attention is caught by something outside.* RUTH *comes back with a mug of milk.*)

NAOMI (*her back to the room*). Is that Ernie Briggs at the bottom of the field now ?

(RUTH *stops in her tracks so suddenly that some of the milk slops over the side of the mug.* NAOMI *turns.*)

NAOMI. I say there's someone at the bottom of the field—is it Ernie ?

RUTH. Probably.

NAOMI. Really, Ruth, I don't know why you let him hang about the place. Here, give that to me ! (*She takes the mug out of* RUTH'S *trembling hand.*) I shouldn't say he's above stealing eggs.

RUTH. Oh no—he wouldn't do that—he knows I trust him.

NAOMI. Then what's he doing there now ?

RUTH. I—I don't know. Maybe it's something to do with that fox.

NAOMI. Is the pen quite secure ?

RUTH (*vaguely*). Pardon ?

NAOMI. The bottom pen. You went down to make sure it was properly fastened.

RUTH. Yes—oh yes. It's alright.

NAOMI (*looking at her sharply*). Aren't you feeling well, Ruth ?

RUTH. Yes—why ?

NAOMI. You're looking pale. Have you got a headache ?

RUTH. I'm alright.

NAOMI. Good. Well, you'd better get off, hadn't you ?

RUTH. Yes. (*She puts on her new mackintosh in a spiritless way.*)

NAOMI. I'll take Ba up at ten, shall I ?

RUTH (*picking up her bag and gloves from the dresser*). Er—yes.

NAOMI. Or will you be back by then ?

RUTH. I don't know. (*She moves to the outer door, then pauses, with her back to the audience.*) Naomi ?

NAOMI (*watching her unsatisfied*). Well ?

RUTH. Which way did you come from the Grange ?

NAOMI. Through the village—the fields were too muddy after the rain. Why ?

RUTH. Nothing. I just wondered.

(NAOMI *looks at her, but there is never any contact between them. There is the sound of a heavy vehicle in the distance.*)

NAOMI. That's the bus coming up the hill. You'll have to run if you want to catch it.

RUTH. Yes. Goodbye. (*A fraction of a pause.*) Kiss Peter for me.

(*She goes, closing the door behind her and her footsteps disappear down the lane.*)

(NAOMI *stands a moment still dissatisfied, then* PETER'S *voice calls from above* " Grandma—hurry up." (NAOMI *goes to the foot of stairs.*)

NAOMI. Shsh ! I'm just coming.

(*She exits.*)

(*The stage is deserted for a few minutes. Sounds of Peter's excited voice from above. There is a gentle knock at the door. It is repeated and then the door opens, and* MISS MITCHUM-BROWNE *comes in. She is a very refined little spinster. Her clothes are old and shabby, but she has done her best to smarten them up. The result is a hotch-potch of bits of lace, black velvet ribbon, and odd pieces of Victorian jewellery. She has a nervous, jerky manner, with a bird-like curiosity. Finding the room empty but lighted, she gives a surprised little exclamation and goes to the house door.)*

Miss M-B. (*calling*). Is anyone in ?
Naomi (*off*). Who's that ?
Miss M-B. It's me, dear. Am I in the way ?
Naomi (*off*). Oh, is that you, Miss Browne ? I'll be down in a minute.

(Miss Mitchum-Browne looks around the room and sighs. She goes to the mantelpiece, runs her finger along the edge and examines it carefully. It is dusty. She sighs again, and stirs the fire delicately with the tip of her shoe. Naomi comes in at the house door. Her expression suggests that she is none too pleased to see the visitor but has her feelings well under control.)

Naomi. Oh hello, Miss Browne. I thought you were up at Clifton Manor to-night ?
Miss M-B. Oh, my dear—haven't you heard ? The most awful thing. The meeting's been postponed. They've had a burglary.
Naomi. At Clifton Manor ?
Miss M-B. Yes, indeed. Poor Lady Bracken ! I feel so sorry for her. But I've always thought it foolish of her not to keep all those diamonds in the Bank ! And her furs too ! But of course they're terribly rich, aren't they ?
Naomi. When was this ?
Miss M-B. Last night, my dear. They were playing bridge at the time and never heard a thing. Wasn't it dreadful ? I felt quite sure you'd have heard about it.
Naomi. No, not a thing. Have they caught the man ?
Miss M-B. No, I don't think so—and I think it was a gang—not just a burglar. Armed too, so they say. It's made me feel quite nervous to be alone in my little place, so I said to myself " I'll just run along and see if Mrs. Martyn is at Oak Cottage "—knowing that Thursday is usually your night—and having seen the young people going down the lane for the bus. . . . Such a smart new mackintosh Ruth was wearing !
Naomi. No you didn't. Only Ruth went for the bus. Chris went by car earlier. But do sit down.
Miss M-B. (*as she sits*). Really ? I could have sworn I saw the two of them together.

NAOMI. Must have been someone else. Oh!

MISS M-B. What's the matter, dear?

NAOMI. Nothing really—I caught sight of someone at the bottom of the field just before Ruth went. She said it was probable Ernie Briggs—so I dare say he walked down the lane with her.

MISS M-B. (*with a little tinkle of laughter*). Oh dear! She makes such a pet of him, doesn't she? Poor Ernie!

NAOMI. She's the only person who's managed to make him remember an errand as far as the village shops. I think she finds him quite useful.

MISS M-B. Just fancy! Of course it shows a very nice spirit, doesn't it? It makes me quite ashamed of myself—but I just can't bear him near me—he's so dirty, isn't he? (*Another laugh.*) I don't know what the dear Vicar would say if he heard me talking like that!

(NAOMI *is wishing she could have a quiet read. Conversation flags for a second.*)

(*Who has every intention of staying for the evening.*) So Ruth's gone to Maidstone by herself, has she?

NAOMI. She's meeting Sally Morgan for a film. Chris has gone to his Old Boys' Dinner.

MISS M-B. Oh, I see. She and Sally are quite friendly, aren't they?

NAOMI (*getting some knitting*). Yes—the four of them seem to get on very well.

MISS M-B. Isn't that nice. A bit surprising really!

NAOMI. Why?

MISS M-B. Well, wasn't Sally engaged to Chris at one time?

NAOMI. That old story! No, I don't think it was anything more than a boy and girl affair—and Sally married Dick years before Ruth came into the picture.

MISS M-B. (*looking at her sideways*). I expect you'd have liked that—wouldn't you? I mean if Chris and Sally had made a match of it.

NAOMI. Oh, at the time I dare say. But it's such ancient history I'd almost forgotten about it.

MISS M-B. (*confidentially*). You're quite happy about this marriage, aren't you, dear?

NAOMI (*carefully*). Why shouldn't I be?

Miss M-B. Oh, no reason at all—and they're very happy—aren't they ?

Naomi. Yes.

Miss M-B. And the children are sweet. It's lovely to see a really united family in this Modern Age—it's so rare, isn't it ?

Naomi. Is it ? Yes, I suppose it is.

Miss M-B. I think Chris is so *wise* to let her go off on her own sometimes.

Naomi (*bored*). It's Chris who's gone off on the loose to-night—one can hardly call the pictures in Maidstone riotous living for a girl who works as hard as Ruth does !

Miss M-B. Now you're laughing at me ! I know I'm old-fashioned—but we were brought up so very differently, weren't we ? Poor Mother never liked *me* to be out alone after dark 'til the day she died.

(Naomi *does the faintest double-take.*)

But then, of course, Ruth's a Londoner, isn't she ?

Naomi. I believe so. (*She puts a skein of wool over Miss Mitchum-Browne's hands.*) D'you mind ?

Miss M-B. (*as if the fact explained everything*). Ah ! (*She looks sideways at Naomi, who doesn't respond.*) I expect that's why she makes up so heavily ?

Naomi. Most girls do nowadays.

Miss M-B. Yes, I suppose they do. (*The tinkling laugh.*) My old-fashioned ideas again ! Mother never liked it. She always used to remark on it—in Ruth, I mean. (*Another expectant pause.*) But I suppose you've got quite used to it ?

Naomi (*briskly*). I think Ruth's pretty enough without it—but if she thinks lipstick improves on nature, that's her business !

Miss M-B. Oh, I think you're so wise to take that attitude ! Yes, I suppose she is rather pretty—NOT so aristocratic looking as Sally—but then the Leylands were so very county, weren't they ?

(*No response from* Naomi.)

Wasn't she called Ruby when first she came here—Ruth, I mean ?

Naomi. Yes.

Miss M-B. Ruby ! Oh dear ! (*Another laugh.*)

Naomi (*exasperated*). She hated the name herself—so Chris decided that as I was Naomi, she should be Ruth.

Miss M-B. Oh, that's charming—charming! Ruth and Naomi—isn't that nice! One of my favourite Bible stories—and I'm sure you both live up to it!

(*Another slight pause.*)

Miss M-B. Do you know Ruth's family?

Naomi. She hasn't one.

Miss M-B. An orphan?

Naomi. I believe so.

Miss M-B. Oh, poor thing! No brothers or sisters?

Naomi. Not so far as I know.

Miss M-B. (*cautiously*). She hadn't been married before, had she, dear?

Naomi. Good gracious no! She only had her twenty-first birthday six months after she married Chris.

Miss M-B. That's what I thought—only. . . .

Naomi (*fixing* Miss Mitchum-Browne *with her eye*). Only what?

Miss M-B. (*slightly flustered*). Oh nothing, dear—it was only something Nurse Beeston said. . . .

Naomi. That woman!

Miss M-B. Yes, she is rather awful, isn't she? And such a gossip! One shouldn't really believe anything she says—but I just thought perhaps if Ruth had been married before it might explain it. . . .

Naomi (*dangerously*). It might explain what?

Miss M-B. (*deciding discretion is the better part of valour*). No, dear—no! I talk too much, don't I? I must remember those three dear little monkeys!

Naomi. Monkeys?

Miss M-B. Yes—you know, see no evil, hear no evil, speak no evil. Sweet! Poor Mother gave them to me years ago—they're on my bookshelf to this day—(*She sighs heavily and looks round the room. She is not attending to the wool, which gets tangled.*) They always used to stand there. (*She points to the mantelpiece.*) Ruth doesn't care for ornaments, does she?

Naomi (*removing wool*). Please don't bother. I don't suppose she's time to dust them! Or the mantel-piece either, by the look of it!

Miss M-B. D'you like the way they've got this house?

Naomi. They did the best they could—there wasn't much money to spare—.

MISS M-B. Of course, we had more furniture, so it looked sort of *cosier*, if you know what I mean.

NAOMI (*at screaming point*). It wasn't a chicken farm-cum-nursery in your days! Look, I'm just going to have a cup of Ovaltine and a boiled egg—would you care to join me?

MISS M-B (*eagerly*). Oh, that's too kind—if it isn't too much bother?

NAOMI (*wearily*). No bother at all—I'll go and get it.

(*She is on the point of escaping for a second when the telephone bell rings.*)

MISS M-B. (*jumping*). Oh, dear—what a shock! That burglary's made me so nervous. . . .

(NAOMI *goes to the telephone*—MISS MITCHUM-BROWNE *listens in with goggling curiosity.*)

NAOMI. Hello? No, Ruth's out, this is. . . . Oh hello, Sally. I didn't recognize your voice. Are you speaking from Maidstone? . . . Why, what's wrong? . . . Oh dear, poor little chap—nothing serious, I hope? . . . No—No—of course you couldn't. . . . Oh yes, my dear, she went ages ago, she caught the 6.40 bus—she was meeting you at the cinema, wasn't she? . . . Mm . . . a bit awkward, I don't quite see what we can do. Would it be any use ringing The Granada? Well, you could try. . . . Yes, do that, Sally, but don't worry if they can't contact her—she'll probably come straight home. Shall I get her to give you a ring when she gets back? All right, my dear— I do hope Timmie's better in the morning. Goodbye. (*She rings off.*)

MISS M-B. (*all agog*). Whatever's happened?

NAOMI. Nothing very serious—Timmie's been sick and is running a temperature, so Sally couldn't get away.

MISS M-B. (*preparing to make a drama of it*). Oh, poor Ruth— what *will* she do?

NAOMI (*ringing down the curtain firmly*). If she's any sense she'll have a quiet sleep in the pictures by herself—I'll go and make our Ovaltine.

(*She marches towards the kitchen door as* THE CURTAIN FALLS.)

ACT I

SCENE 2. (*Friday*)

Twenty-four hours later. The room is untidier than ever. CHRIS
*has mixed chicken food, and left trails of it, including an empty
pail, about the place. He has also got himself odd cups of tea,
and snatched meals. He is now outside the window, sawing
wood. The saw makes an agitated, discordant sound for a few
seconds, and then the telephone bell rings.* CHRIS *comes in through
the outer door, and moves eagerly towards it. He is in shabby
working clothes with gum boots—unshaven, and smoking the butt
end of a cigarette.*

CHRIS (*at 'phone*). Hello—hello—yes ? (*A note of disappointment comes into his voice.*) Oh, hello, Mother—I thought perhaps
it might be the police. No—not a blasted thing since this morning.
How are the kids ? Fine. Peter isn't fretting, is he ? Good.
Oh, I'm all right—but I can't say I'm enjoying myself. The
waiting's pretty grim. No—don't do that—you stay with the
children. I'll be all right—honest. I've sawn up enough logs
to-day to see us through the winter ! I'll ring you again later.
'Bye.

(*He rings off and moves restlessly to the mantelpiece. He throws his
cigarette into the grate, and lights another from a half-empty
packet. As he is doing so,* MISS MITCHUM-BROWNE *passes the
window, and appears in the outer-door, which* CHRIS *has left open.*)

MISS M-B. My dear boy, I've only just heard your news—I
had to go into Maidstone to-day, and have only just got back.
May I come in a moment ?

CHRIS (*reluctantly*). Oh—do. I'm afraid the place is in rather
a mess.

MISS M-B. Don't apologize, please. As I got off the bus I met
Mrs. Foster and she said to me " Have you heard ? Young Mrs.
Martyn is missing." Well, you could have knocked me down
with a feather ! Why I was here until nearly ten o'clock last

night with your dear mother, and she was expecting Ruth back at any moment. What happened ?

CHRIS. She just didn't turn up. I suppose it's all round the village by now ?

MISS M-B. But of course ! And I was here when Sally 'phoned up to say she couldn't meet Ruth in Maidstone. Her little boy's got measles, Mrs. Foster said—Dr. Foster has been up there this morning. You've been on to the police of course ?

CHRIS. Naturally.

MISS M-B. And no news so far ?

CHRIS. No.

MISS M-B. What can have happened to her ?

CHRIS (*pulling himself together with an effort*). There's probably some quite obvious explanation—loss of memory or something.

MISS M-B. Well, I admire you for keeping so calm—I do really.

CHRIS. It's no good panicking. (*He repeats wearily.*) I expect there's an explanation.

MISS M-B. What time did you get back ?

CHRIS. I dunno—just after midnight I think.

MISS M-B. Your poor mother—she must have been quite desperate. She'd waited of course ?

CHRIS. Of course. She stayed the night and took the kids up to the Grange this morning.

MISS M-B. How like her ! She's so fond of Ruth—isn't she ? (*She looks at him sideways.*)

CHRIS (*ignoring this*). Peter loves being with Hannah— they're all right.

MISS M-B. Of course they are—don't you worry about that. Well, dear me, there's certainly some excitement in Fellinge at the moment—first the burglary at Clifton Manor—and now this.

CHRIS. Burglary ?

MISS M-B. Oh dear—how tactless of me ! I'm so sorry— didn't you know ?

CHRIS. No. When was that ?

MISS M-B. Two nights ago, but I don't suppose the incidents could be in any way connected.

CHRIS. Why should they be ?

MISS M-B. No—no—of course not. Stupid of me to mention it.

(*For a second* CHRIS *looks as if he'd like to brain her, but again pulls himself together.*)

CHRIS. I should have heard later, but I haven't been in the village to-day.

MISS M-B. Naturally, my dear boy—I don't suppose you dare leave this house in case Ruth comes back ?

CHRIS. I left it this morning to go into Maidstone and see the police.

MISS M-B. And what did they say ?

CHRIS. They took particulars—but they weren't very interested.

MISS M-B. And you've heard nothing since ?

CHRIS. No.

MISS M-B. What a pity Sally was detained last night. You would at least know if Ruth got to Maidstone.

CHRIS (*more and more fed up*). Well we don't.

MISS M-B. No—no—of course not. Silly of me ! Well, it's all terribly worrying for you. I do wish I could do something to help.

CHRIS. Very kind of you, but . . .

MISS M-B. Perhaps you'd allow me to tidy up for you ? (*Coyly.*) I know you men are so helpless !

CHRIS. No—really—thank you.

MISS M-B. Well, let me get you something to eat ? Or a nice cup of tea perhaps ?

CHRIS (*beginning to get desperate*). No—please don't bother about me. (*With a slightly shaking hand he lights another cigarette from the one he's been smoking.*)

MISS M-B (*playfully*). Naughty ! You know you're smoking too much !

(*He is practically at the end of his tether, but to his intense relief,* NAOMI *walks in through the open door.*)

CHRIS (*his relief in his voice*). Oh hello, Mother !

(NAOMI *catches the look in his eye and deals with the situation briskly.*)

NAOMI. Oh there you are, Miss Browne—I thought you must be at home as I saw a light in your front room as I passed.

MISS M-B. (*panicking at once*). A light ! But there's nobody there !

NAOMI. Perhaps you left it on yourself.

Miss M-B.   But it wasn't dark when I left !

Naomi.   Well, it's getting dark now. (*She moves over and switches on the light.*)

Miss M-B.   Oh good gracious—I'd better go and see what's happened—what *is* going on in this village ? You will excuse me, both of you, won't you ?

Naomi.   Yes, you run along. I'll call in on my way back to make sure all's well.

Miss M-B.   Oh thank you—thank you. (*She goes up to the door and turns.*) And you'll let me have your news as soon as you hear ?

Naomi.   Of course.

(Miss Mitchum-Browne *trots out and her footsteps disappear down the lane.* Naomi *shuts the door and draws the curtains.*)

Chris.   Thank you, Mother—you saved my life ! *Was* there a light in her front room ?

Naomi.   No ! I hope she doesn't come back to tell me I was mistaken ! (*She automatically begins to tidy up the room.*)

Chris.   I'd no idea you were such a good liar ! I told you not to come.

Naomi.   Lucky I did, wasn't it ? The children are perfectly all right with Hannah, so I thought I'd come over and be with you for a bit. Have you had anything to eat to-day ? (*She looks at a dirty cup and half a loaf of stale bread on the table.*)

Chris.   Yes—I think so. . . .

Naomi.   Looks very appetizing, I must say ! I've brought you some sandwiches and a drop of brandy. (*She produces them from her basket.*)

Chris.   I'm all right.

Naomi (*briskly*).   Well, you don't look it ! You'd probably feel better for a shave.

Chris (*feeling his chin*).   Sorry—I forgot. I'll have one presently.

Naomi.   Never mind—let me give you a drink.

Chris.   No thanks.

Naomi.   Well sit down and have something to eat, while I tidy up this room.

Chris.   All you women ever want to do is to tidy up ! I've just told Mitchum-B. to leave it alone.

Naomi.   It looks even more sordid than usual. Sit down ! (*He*

does so. She hands him the packet of sandwiches, and he makes a
pretence of eating them while they talk.) Now—tell me exactly what's
been happening ?

CHRIS. Nothing's been happening ! To-day's seemed like a
week.

NAOMI. I expect it has. But you know, Christopher, hundreds
of people are reported missing every year for one reason or
another.

CHRIS. Possibly—hundreds aren't my Ruth.

NAOMI. No. (*A pause.*) What exactly did the police say ?

CHRIS. There was nothing to say—except take particulars.

NAOMI. But did they suggest anything helpful ?

CHRIS. No. They turned up a list of street accidents—but
there'd only been one last night, and that was a man. They
asked about her health—if she was likely to lose her memory.
Then they told me to get home in case she turned up.

NAOMI. D'you think she was ?

CHRIS. Was what ?

NAOMI. Likely to lose her memory ?

CHRIS. How on earth should I know ?

NAOMI. I mean has she had any headaches, or been worried
about anything lately ?

CHRIS. Not as far as I know.

NAOMI. Actually, I rather wondered if she had a headache last
night.

CHRIS (*quickly*). Why ? Didn't you think she looked well ?

NAOMI. A bit pale—but then she often is, isn't she ?

CHRIS. Perhaps she shouldn't have gone out. I was so busy
getting off myself I never noticed. Perhaps . . .

NAOMI. Oh I don't think it was anything serious. I asked her
if she had one, as a matter of fact, and she said no. I'm just
trying to probe the mystery, and remember exactly what
happened before she went.

CHRIS. She left soon after I did ?

NAOMI. Yes. (*Thinking back.*) I came down to get some
milk for Peter—she was emptying money out of that vase, and
putting it in her purse. . . .

CHRIS. Oh Lord—I forgot to ask her if she had enough. (*He
rises, and gets the vase from the mantelpiece.*) But I think there
was about £4 egg money here. (*He looks in vase.*) Apparently she
took the lot !

NAOMI. Would she need all that ?

CHRIS. No—there couldn't have been as much as I thought. (*He puts vase back, and returns to the table.*) Then what ?

NAOMI. I asked for the milk, and she went and fetched it from the kitchen. Yes—she did seem a bit nervous—I remember she slopped some over as she was handing it to me.

CHRIS. Then something *had* happened to upset her. Had you been having a row with her ?

NAOMI (*crisply*). Don't be silly ! Am I in the habit of having rows with your wife ?

CHRIS. You're a bit of a gorgon sometimes !

NAOMI. Don't talk nonsense—and for heaven's sake sit down and have a drink !

CHRIS. I think perhaps I will. (*He gets a glass from the sideboard, and pours himself out a small tot*). Will you have one ?

NAOMI. No thanks. You'd better have a cigarette too. (*She crosses to the mantelpiece, and fetches a half empty packet.*) The sandwiches don't seem to interest you.

CHRIS (*taking cigarette, which she lights for him*). I'm not hungry. That's my third packet of fags to-day.

NAOMI. Lucky this doesn't happen often, or you'd soon be bankrupt !

CHRIS (*continuing his train of thought*). She seemed perfectly all right when I left—what *could* have happened to upset her in those last five minutes ?

NAOMI. I don't see how anything could—she just went down the field to close the pen.

CHRIS. But I saw her after that.

NAOMI. Yes—we're obviously not getting anywhere.

CHRIS. No. (*He gulps down his brandy, and pours himself another.*)

NAOMI. That is purely medicinal—don't overdo it !

CHRIS. If you imagine two minute tots are going to make me paralytic, you're mistaken !

NAOMI. It's very chilly in here—shall I light a fire ?

CHRIS. If you like. I'll go and get some logs. (*He rises, and moves to outer door. As he opens it,* ERNIE BRIGGS *practically falls into the room.* ERNIE *is young, and dressed in a hotch-potch of dirty clothes. He is not very bright.*)

CHRIS. What the hell are you doing there ?

ERNIE. She's lorst, ben't she ?

CHRIS. Who's lost ?

ERNIE. The Lady.

CHRIS (*more gently*). Don't worry, Ernie. She'll soon be back.

ERNIE. I seen 'er.

CHRIS. When did you see her ?

ERNIE. S'morning.

CHRIS. No, Ernie—not this morning. You came round for the shopping list—don't you remember ? And she wasn't here.

ERNIE (*firmly*). I *seen* 'er.

NAOMI. I know what he means, Chris. Miss Browne said she saw him walking down the lane with Ruth last night—he's probably thinking of that.

CHRIS. I'm not so sure. Come in a moment, Ernie, and shut the door.

(*A happy smile spreads over* ERNIE'S *face. He shuts the door with great care, and shuffles in.*)

ERNIE (*looking round eagerly*). She gives Oi beer 'ere !

CHRIS. Never mind about that now. We want to talk to you.

ERNIE (*with a sigh*). She trusts Oi. Oi do 'er shoppin' for 'er.

CHRIS. Yes—yes—I know you do. You're fond of her, aren't you ?

ERNIE (*with great pride*). She trusts Oi !

CHRIS. Of course she does—and so do we. Now, you say you saw her ?

ERNIE. S'roight.

CHRIS. But it couldn't have been this morning, because she wasn't here when you came. You really mean you walked down the lane with her last night, don't you ?

ERNIE. No—not down the lane. But I *seen* 'er.

CHRIS. But Miss Brown said she saw you walking down the lane together.

ERNIE (*with contempt*). She ! She don't know nothin'. I seen *my* lady !

NAOMI. You're merely wasting time, Christopher. Give him some beer and let him go.

ERNIE. Oi get beer 'ere !

CHRIS. Wait a minute, Mother. I believe there's something behind this. You shall have some beer in a minute, old son—but you've got to try and think first. (ERNIE *gives a gusty sigh.*) Now —you tell us where you saw her. Was it dark ?

ERNIE (*after careful thought*). S'roight ! It were dark.

CHRIS. Then you *do* mean last night ?

ERNIE. S'roight.

CHRIS.   But you didn't walk down the lane with her ?

ERNIE.   No—she were with 'im.

CHRIS.   Him ?   Who d'you mean ?

ERNIE.   Oi dunno.

NAOMI.   He's got it all muddled, Chris. . . .

CHRIS.   Oh leave this to me, Mother !   Think Ernie—think very hard ?

ERNIE (*an inspiration*).   There were the bus !

CHRIS.   I know—you mean you saw her at the bus stop ?

ERNIE (*delighted with himself*).   S'roight.   She were talkin'.

CHRIS.   She was standing at the bus stop, talking to somebody (ERNIE *nods*).   Now we're getting somewhere !   Was it anyone in the village, Ernie ?

ERNIE.   No—she were talking'.

CHRIS.   Did she get on the bus ?

ERNIE.   It went down the 'ill.   She were *talkin'*.   (*He is a little too insistent about this.*)

NAOMI.   So we gather !

CHRIS.   Did you speak to her, Ernie ?

ERNIE.   No—she were . . .

NAOMI.   Talking !   For heaven's sake, Chris, you're not getting anywhere.

CHRIS.   Perhaps I am.   It seems to me Ruth never got to Maidstone at all, which surely might be important.   I think you deserve your beer, Ernie.

ERNIE (*pointing delightedly*).   She kep' it there !

CHRIS.   How right you are !   (*He gets out a bottle, and gives it to* ERNIE.)

ERNIE (*hugging the bottle to him*).   All for Oi ?

CHRIS.   All for you.   Now run along.   But go straight home, like a good boy.   Bessie'll be worried.

(ERNIE *hastens to the outer door before* CHRIS *can change his mind— but at the last minute he turns round.*)

ERNIE (*firmly*).   Oi seen 'er !   (*He exits, and* CHRIS *shuts the door.*)

CHRIS.   I believe Ruth did miss that bus, Mother.

NAOMI.   Ernie's been missing it for twenty years !   One of his favourite pastimes is standing on that corner directing the traffic !   I doubt if the police would consider him a very reliable witness.

CHRIS (*slowly*). What d'you think he meant when he said Ruth was walking down the lane with " him " ?

NAOMI. Oh, it might have been anyone in the village. I shouldn't worry about that.

CHRIS. But I do worry. That silly old woman said something about a burglary at Clifton Manor. Such awful things happen nowadays.

NAOMI. My dear boy—I think that's rather letting your imagination run away with you !

CHRIS. I wish to God the police would ring up. (*He goes back to table, and helps himself to a third tot of brandy, which he gulps down.*)

NAOMI (*watching him anxiously*). Please try and relax, my dear—it's no good working yourself into a state.

CHRIS (*his tongue loosened by the brandy*). Why should you worry ? You don't care about Ruth anyway !

NAOMI. What d'you mean ?

CHRIS. Well, you've never liked her, have you ?

NAOMI (*carefully*). I've never known her well enough either to like or dislike her.

CHRIS. Why not ?

NAOMI. D'you consider either of you has invited it ?

CHRIS. You mean we've been secretive ?

NAOMI. Well I wouldn't say you've exactly encouraged intimacy ! It's five years since you brought Ruth to Fellinge. I was given exactly seven days' notice that you were going to be married, and wasn't even invited to the Register Office ! I tried to take it in my stride. I raised money that I could ill afford to help you rent this place, and buy the first lot of chickens. After which, it was made pretty plain by both of you, that if I'd mind my own business, you'd mind yours !

CHRIS. We did nothing of the kind ! Anyway, Ruth didn't think you wanted to be intimate. She got the impression that you thought her inferior.

NAOMI. I consider that *most* unfair, Christopher ! I've tried again and again to talk to Ruth, and find out something about her—and every time it was like running into a stone wall.

CHRIS. Why should you want to find out about her ?

NAOMI. Because she happens to be my daughter-in-law ! D'you think it's been amusing to live within a stone's throw of you, my only child, and to be treated like a complete stranger ?

I've no desire to be either a possessive mother, or an interfering in-law—but there is a happy medium !

CHRIS. Well I'm sorry—we haven't meant it like that.

NAOMI. I dare say not—you've just been too selfishly pre-occupied with your own lives to bother about mine. Of course, I have been allowed to come and baby-sit this last year—so I suppose I should be grateful for small mercies !

CHRIS. I'd no idea you felt like that—you never said so !

NAOMI. Aren't men wonderful ! I suppose it never struck you that there might be gossip about my son's mysterious marriage in the village ?

CHRIS. It isn't the least mysterious !

NAOMI. I'm glad to hear it ! Perhaps, in the present circumstances, you'll allow me to know one or two things about Ruth ?

CHRIS. What about her ?

NAOMI. Anything ! Who is she, for a start ?

CHRIS. Are you enquiring into her social background ?

NAOMI. No—I'm not ! I just want to know something of her history. She's a Londoner, isn't she ?

CHRIS. Yes.

NAOMI. Do you know her parents ?

CHRIS. No—they were both dead when I met her.

NAOMI. Has she any family ?

CHRIS. No.

NAOMI. She was living alone in London ?

CHRIS. Yes.

NAOMI. What was she doing ?

CHRIS. Shorthand typing—she loathed it.

NAOMI. You once said you picked her up on a train—were you joking ?

CHRIS. No. She picked me up on a train—literally !

NAOMI. Oh ?

CHRIS. My leg was still stiff in those days, and I walked with a stick. I tripped and fell into a train at Victoria, and she fielded me.

NAOMI. Oh—I see !

CHRIS. Naturally, we got into conversation.

NAOMI. Naturally !

CHRIS. There you are, you see !

NAOMI. Go on—when did you meet her next ?

CHRIS. At Lyons' Corner House two days later. I asked her to marry me.

NAOMI. Did she accept you ?

CHRIS. No—she said we didn't know each other well enough.

NAOMI. Did she indeed !

CHRIS. I suppose it all sounds cracked to you that I should look at a girl who gave me a helping hand in a train, and know I wanted to marry her ?

NAOMI. I want to understand, Christopher—don't you see I'm trying to understand. I just want you to talk to me as if I were a relation of yours !

CHRIS. What the hell's the good ? You could never understand. There are aeons between your generation and mine— aeons and aeons ! What's the good of talking about the past ? It's now that matters ! Ruth's lost—I don't know where she is, and it's driving me crazy ! I couldn't live without her now. She means everything to me—everything ! Call it selfish if you like— but isn't my blasted generation entitled to a little stability ? (*He pulls himself together suddenly.*) I shouldn't have had that brandy !

NAOMI (*quietly, because she's hurt*). Perhaps not.

CHRIS. I'm sorry, Mother.

NAOMI. It doesn't matter.

CHRIS. Oh why can I talk to Ruth, and not to you ?

NAOMI. Possibly because we didn't meet on a train !

(*Any contact they might have had evaporates.*)

CHRIS. I was going to get some logs for the fire !

(*He moves towards the outer door, as he does so the sound of a car is heard coming up the lane. NAOMI moves swiftly to the window, and looks through the closed curtains.*)

NAOMI. I think this may be news.

(*The car has stopped outside.*)

CHRIS (*following her to the window*). Is Ruth there ?

NAOMI. No—but it looks like a police car. Let them in.

(CHRIS *goes to the door and opens it.* INSPECTOR THORNTON *is standing outside.*)

THORNTON. Mr. Martyn ?

CHRIS. Yes.

THORNTON. May I come in a moment ?

(CHRIS *lets him pass into the room.*)

CHRIS. This is my mother.

THORNTON. Good evening.

NAOMI. Good evening.

THORNTON. My name's Thornton of the County Constabulary.

CHRIS. You've come about my wife ?

THORNTON. Yes—there are one or two points I wish to check up. I thought it best to come and have a chat with you.

(*He is watching* CHRIS *keenly as he talks, as if sizing up the man with whom he has to deal.*)

CHRIS (*eagerly*). Yes ?

NAOMI. Would you prefer to talk to my son alone, Inspector ?

THORNTON. No, Mrs. Martyn—I'd prefer you to remain.

NAOMI. Very well—won't you sit down ?

THORNTON. Thank you. (*He and* NAOMI *sit.*)

CHRIS. Well ? Have you any definite news ?

THORNTON. It's difficult to say. D'you mind if I just clear up one or two things first—and then I'll tell you what's been happening as far as we're concerned.

CHRIS. But have you any def—— ?

THORNTON. One moment, please.

CHRIS (*possessing his soul in patience*). Very well.

THORNTON (*consulting notes*). Your wife was five foot four, fresh complexion and fair hair. Wearing a red mackintosh over a navy skirt and white blouse ?

CHRIS. I think that's what she was wearing.

NAOMI. Yes she was. A new red mackintosh. Black high-heeled shoes and nylon stockings. No hat.

THORNTON (*with a smile*). Thank you—the ladies are generally more correct about these things ! I think you told us, Mr. Martyn, that she was going into Maidstone to meet a friend, who was detained at the last moment ?

CHRIS. Yes.

THORNTON. Do you think it likely that, not finding her friend at the meeting place, your wife might have accepted a lift from a car coming in this direction ?

CHRIS. Very unlikely I should say.

THORNTON. She wouldn't have accepted a lift from a stranger ?

CHRIS. Good Lord no ! She'd run a mile if anyone tried to pick her up !

NAOMI. Chris, I think perhaps you'd better tell the Inspector about Ernie.

THORNTON. What was that ?

CHRIS. I doubt if it's very important.

THORNTON. Everything is important, Mr. Martyn.

CHRIS. Well we've just had a visit from a somewhat dubious witness, who insists he saw her talking to someone at the end of the lane here when the bus went by.

THORNTON. Ah—now that is important. (*He makes a note.*) Who told you this ? I'd like to see him.

NAOMI. Ernie's the village simpleton—but very devoted to my daughter-in-law. Have you checked up as to whether she did travel on the 6.40 ?

THORNTON. We have, of course, contacted the conductor on duty—but he was new on the route and the bus was very crowded. He thought the young lady was a passenger, but wasn't certain. If we could make sure one way or another, it would be a help in linking up with some other information that came to hand to-day.

CHRIS. What was that ?

THORNTON. Well, sir, one of our men on duty in Week Street, Maidstone, last night was watching a car that had been parked too long. When the owner returned he was talking to a young lady answering to the description you had given us.

CHRIS. What time was that ?

THORNTON. About eight o'clock. That's why I asked if Mrs. Martyn might have accepted a lift.

CHRIS. Did this girl get into the car then ?

THORNTON. Yes. They drove off in the Ashford direction.

NAOMI. That might have been the time she'd have been returning, Christopher, if she didn't stay and see the film.

THORNTON (*watching them keenly*). Did this man—Ernie—say who she was talking to at the bus stop ?

CHRIS. No. I don't think it was anyone he knew.

THORNTON. Nobody in the village then ?

CHRIS. No—but the poor old boy's so hazy—I don't think we can consider him very reliable.

THORNTON. No, sir. (*A pause.*) Either way it would appear that Mrs. Martyn was talking to a stranger ?

CHRIS. It looks like that—but it's so unlike her, I can't help feeling you're barking up the wrong tree.

THORNTON. Two wrong trees, Mr. Martyn ?

(*His voice is so grave that* CHRIS *realizes something is wrong.*)

CHRIS. You've some more information, haven't you ?

THORNTON. Yes I have. But I don't yet know that it's in any way connected with you.

CHRIS. Tell me.

THORNTON. The young woman that our man Gregg saw last night has just been found.

CHRIS. Found ? Where ?

THORNTON. Not far from Ashford, sir.

CHRIS. My God, why didn't you say so ? Is it my wife ?

THORNTON. We don't know. (*Rising.*) We want you, if you will, to come along now and—identify her.

CHRIS. Identify her ?

(NAOMI *realizes what he's driving at. She rises swiftly and goes to* CHRIS'S *side.*)

THORNTON. Take it easy if you can, Mr. Martyn. I hope you're right, and we are barking up the wrong tree. The girl we've found is dead.

CURTAIN.

END OF ACT I.

ACT II

Saturday Morning

(*Rain is pouring down heavily outside, and can be heard lashing against the window. NAOMI, in an overall, is clearing up the room—dusting and generally putting it to rights. A car is heard coming up the lane and stopping. THORNTON passes the window. NAOMI sees him and opens the door before he has time to knock.*)

NAOMI. Good morning, Inspector. You'd better come inside quickly.

THORNTON. Thank you, Mrs. Martyn. Terrible weather, isn't it ?

NAOMI. It never stopped pouring all night. Fortunately my son slept through it. He was in such a state when he arrived home after identifying his wife that I took it on myself to call in the family doctor, who gave him a strong bromide. He's slept for nearly fifteen hours.

THORNTON. I'm glad. Is he awake now ?

NAOMI. Yes—I heard him moving about a few minutes ago. Do you want to see him ?

THORNTON. Yes—I did rather want a word with him. But I wouldn't want to disturb him if he was resting. I'm afraid it's been a terrible shock for him ?

NAOMI. Yes.

THORNTON. A somewhat highly strung gentleman, I imagine ?

NAOMI. He had a bad time in the war, and his nerves weren't good for several years—but he's been all right lately. He was bearing up amazingly until you took him to the mortuary on Friday night.

THORNTON. Ours is not always an easy job.

NAOMI. I'm sure it's not. (*A pause.*) Was he—was he very hysterical ?

THORNTON (*carefully*). It was a grim experience for him, Mrs. Martyn. He was very devoted to his wife ?

NAOMI. Unusually so—for these days !

THORNTON. Ah!

(*Another pause. He looks at* NAOMI, *wondering how far he can question her. She appears remarkably calm.*)

Children ?
NAOMI. Two.
THORNTON. Young ?
NAOMI. A boy of three and a baby girl of four months.
THORNTON. I see. (*He ventures a little further.*) You were satisfied with the marriage yourself ?
NAOMI (*coldly*). Naturally.
THORNTON (*deciding discretion is advisable*). Well, d'you think I might see Mr. Martyn ? The inquest is fixed for Monday morning, and I thought it best if I came along and saw him, rather than 'phoning.
NAOMI. Kind of you. I'll go and see if he's dressed.
THORNTON. Thank you.

(NAOMI *goes upstairs. The rain is still pouring down. Thornton goes to the fire and warms his hands while he is waiting.* ERNIE *appears in the rain outside the window—he wears an old sack over his head and shoulders. Thornton turns at the fire to warm his back and sees him. He crosses to the door and opens it.*)

THORNTON. What d'you want, sonny ?
ERNIE (*coming in to doorway*). She's lorst, ben't she ?
THORNTON. Who's lost ?
ERNIE. The Lady. I seen 'er.
THORNTON. Ah—I know who you are. You're Ernie, aren't you ?
ERNIE. S'roight. I seen 'er !
THORNTON. Yes—and I want to talk to you. Come in a moment.
ERNIE. Oi be wet !
THORNTON. Never mind. I'll take your overcoat for you!

(*He takes the wet sack from* ERNIE, *and propels him gently inside the door.*)

ERNIE (*hesitating on the mat*). She ben't 'ere ?
THORNTON. No—but you can come in. (ERNIE *wipes his feet*

carefully and comes in.) Now! I want you to tell me where you saw her?

ERNIE. You be a copper, ben't you?

THORNTON. That's right—but there's nothing to be afraid of.

ERNIE. Oi ben't afraid. Oi done nothink wrong!

THORNTON. I'm sure you haven't.

ERNIE. She trusts Oi—Oi don't steal eggs!

THORNTON. No. Now you think very carefully, Ernie, and tell me where you saw her.

(ERNIE *looks stubborn.*)

Come along—you want to help, don't you?

ERNIE (*pleased—eagerly*). Oi 'elp the lady. Oi done 'er shoppin' —Oi remember for 'er—she trusts Oi.

THORNTON. Well, that's fine, old son. Now try to remember for me, will you? You saw the lady at the bus stop, didn't you?

ERNIE. S'roight—By bus stop!

THORNTON. You're sure?

(ERNIE *nods vigorously.*)

Did she get on the bus?

ERNIE. It went up the 'ill.

THORNTON. It went up the hill without her?

(ERNIE *nods again.*)

She didn't get on the bus because she was talking to someone?

(ERNIE *looks stubborn again.*)

That's what you told Mr. Martyn, wasn't it?

(*No response.*)

THORNTON. Well, come on, Ernie, that's right, isn't it?

(*No response—*THORNTON *goes on patiently.*)

You want to help, don't you?

(*A nod.*)

Can you remember who she was talking to ?

(ERNIE *shakes his head miserably.*)

It wasn't anybody you knew ?

(ERNIE *looks towards the stairs cautiously—he then looks towards the window in the same way. He moves close to the* INSPECTOR, *and says in a mysterious whisper.*)

ERNIE. She *ben't* talkin'.
THORNTON. Wasn't she, Ernie ? What was she doing then ?

(ERNIE *repeats the same process, then getting even closer to the* INSPECTOR, *he says in his ear.*)

ERNIE. She were kissin'.
THORNTON (*very matter of fact*). Was she, Ernie ?
ERNIE (*in a hoarse whisper*). 'Uggin' and kissin'—Don't you tell *them* !
THORNTON. No, I won't, Ernie. And don't you tell anyone else, will you ?
ERNIE (*with pride*). No—she trusts Oi !
THORNTON. That's it. Just a secret between you and me—eh ?
ERNIE (*nodding his head up and down*). S'roight. A secret ! (*He looks wistfully towards the sideboard.*) Oi get beer 'ere !

(NAOMI *comes down the stairs.*)

NAOMI. What are you doing here, Ernie ?
ERNIE (*patting his nose knowingly*). Oi got 'er secret !
THORNTON. Well you keep it to yourself, old boy ! He's trying to be helpful, Mrs. Martyn.
ERNIE (*proudly*). Helpful !
THORNTON. That's it—and you're not to talk to anyone else— you run along now. (*He puts the sack round Ernie's shoulders.*)

(ERNIE *gives another longing look towards the sideboard, but it's obvious nothing is forthcoming. He gives a gusty sigh, and shuffles off through the outer door.*)

NAOMI (*moving up to close it after him*). My son will be down in a minute, Inspector.

THORNTON. Thank you, Mrs. Martyn.

NAOMI. What was Ernie being so mysterious about ?

THORNTON. I was trying to pump him a little in view of what you told me the other night.

NAOMI. Did you get anything further out of him ?

THORNTON. I don't think so—it's obvious he was very attached to your daughter-in-law ?

NAOMI. Yes—Ruth managed to get more sense out of him than most. His wits are very dim, poor thing, but she seemed to have some means of contact with him. He informed you that she was " talkin' " to someone at the bus stop ?

THORNTON. Yes. I think he must have been mistaken—but he seems very definite on the point.

NAOMI. Yes. (*A pause.*) It's a strange feeling, Inspector.

THORNTON (*not following*). Yes ?

NAOMI. I mean for ordinary law-abiding citizens, such as we are, to be mixed up in a case like this.

THORNTON. Yes—I suppose it is.

NAOMI. The sort of thing one took for granted would never happen. Not that I'd ever really thought about it.

THORNTON. Your son does realize the full implications ?

NAOMI. Oh yes—he's anxious to help you in any way he can.

THORNTON. Good. (*He looks at her calm, detached face.*) I don't want to bother him more than necessary—but circumstances have placed him in a rather important position.

NAOMI. Yes—I see that. (*Another pause.*) He was awake when I went up, and is just getting dressed. I think you'll find him calmer than the last time you saw him. (*There is another slight pause.*)

THORNTON. You were the last person to see your daughter-in-law before she left, weren't you ?

NAOMI. Yes.

THORNTON. Did she seem in any way distraught or worried ?

NAOMI. A little tired perhaps. I never thought her very strong.

THORNTON. No ?

NAOMI. There's a lot of work to do on a chicken farm, you know, and she had the children to look after. She wasn't the tough country type that takes these things in their stride.

THORNTON. A townswoman, was she ?

NAOMI. Yes, I think so.

THORNTON. Ah . . .

(*Enter* CHRIS.)

CHRIS. Good morning, Inspector.

THORNTON. Oh—good morning, Mr. Martyn.

CHRIS. You want to see me ?

THORNTON. If it's convenient, sir.

(CHRIS *moves to the mantelpiece and collects the inevitable packet of cigarettes.*)

NAOMI. I expect you'd like to talk to my son alone ?

THORNTON. If you please, madam.

NAOMI. Very well. I'll be in the kitchen if you want me, Chris.

CHRIS. All right.

(NAOMI *goes through the kitchen door.*)

(*The rain eases off and stops through this scene.*)

CHRIS (*handing packet*). Cigarette ?

THORNTON. Not at the moment, thank you, sir.

(CHRIS *gets one out, and* THORNTON *lights it for him.*)

CHRIS. Well ?

THORNTON (*watching* CHRIS *closely as he talks*). The inquest has been arranged for three o'clock on Monday, in Maidstone Town Hall. I thought I'd call in and make arrangements with you.

CHRIS. Thanks.

THORNTON (*slowly*). Have you ever attended an inquest, Mr. Martyn ?

CHRIS. No—I can't say I'm looking forward to it.

THORNTON. A Coroner's Court is bound to be a bit gruelling for the relatives of the—er—deceased.

CHRIS. So I imagine.

THORNTON. All sorts of questions are asked, and have to be answered.

CHRIS. What sort of questions ?

THORNTON. Sometimes rather intimate ones. (*There is a pause.*) Would you mind if I asked you one or two now ?

CHRIS (*his face set*). If you must—Sit down, won't you ?
THORNTON. Thank you.

(*They both sit.*)

THORNTON. I just want to prepare you for Monday.
CHRIS. Go on—I'm all right.
THORNTON (*after another slight pause*). I wasn't quite certain how much you took in last night ?
CHRIS. Damn little—except that my wife was dead.
THORNTON. You did realize it was a case of murder ?
CHRIS. Pretty obvious, wasn't it ?
THORNTON. And that being so, the Coroner will be more searching than he would be in a more straight forward case ?
CHRIS. I suppose so.
THORNTON. And the Press more interested ?
CHRIS. You're trying to tell me there's going to be a hell of a lot of publicity ?
THORNTON. I'm afraid so, sir.
CHRIS. Oh God.

(*He gets up and throws his cigarette into the grate—he is obviously keeping a tight grip on himself.*)

THORNTON (*still watching him closely*). It might help if you told me a little about Mrs. Martyn now—then I could prepare you—for the sort of things that may be asked.

(CHRIS *pulls himself together and turns to face* THORNTON.)

CHRIS. What d'you want to know ?
THORNTON. Won't you sit down, sir ?

(CHRIS *hesitates—but sits.*)

Mrs. Martyn was a Miss Ruby Smith before her marriage ?
CHRIS. Yes.
THORNTON. That took place about five years ago ?
CHRIS. Five and a half.
THORNTON. Had you known each other long before marriage ?
CHRIS. No—not very long.
THORNTON. How long ?
CHRIS. About eight weeks.

THORNTON. I see. (*Cautiously.*) Did you know her family ?

CHRIS. She had no family.

THORNTON. None at all ?

CHRIS. No—her parents were dead when I met her.

THORNTON. She came from London ?

CHRIS. Yes.

THORNTON. She'd lived there all her life ?

CHRIS. I believe so—she was in an orphanage for a time after she lost her people.

THORNTON. D'you know where it was ?

CHRIS. No—she didn't talk about it. She'd been unhappy— I wanted her to forget the past.

THORNTON. I see. (*He pauses again.*) She'd really told you very little about herself ?

CHRIS (*suddenly shutting up like a clam*). All I wanted to know.

THORNTON. I see. (*Another pause.*) You can help me—and yourself—best by telling me everything you know about Mrs. Martyn.

CHRIS. I'm telling you everything I know. (*He looks sharply at* THORNTON.) What is all this, Inspector ?

THORNTON. If you're trying to shield her, Mr. Martyn, you're serving no useful purpose in the present circumstances.

CHRIS. *Shield* her ? What the devil are you talking about ? We met—casually, if that's what you're getting at. We married soon after because there was no point in waiting. I suppose I didn't know much about her. We'd both been through the mill. She never probed into my life—why should I probe into hers ?

THORNTON. That's all I'm trying to find out.

CHRIS (*getting slightly impatient*). So what ?

THORNTON. I'm afraid the Coroner will be more interested in her past life than you have been.

CHRIS. Why ?

THORNTON. Murders are rarely committed without a motive you know—anything that might lead to a clue will have to be examined.

CHRIS. Well, I can't tell him what I don't know, can I ?

THORNTON. No. (*A pause.*) But others may know more than you do.

CHRIS. Others ? What others ?

THORNTON. It's our job to find your wife's murderer, Mr. Martyn. The inquest is only the beginning. Facts that come out then are going to be enlarged on later.

CHRIS. What facts ? I'm not following you.

THORNTON (*trying a new method of approach*). Have you seen this morning's papers ?

CHRIS. No—I only woke up a quarter of an hour ago. (*Trying to be casual.*) Are they very sensational ?

THORNTON (*slowly*). No—not yet—just the bare facts—and a photograph.

CHRIS (*looking up quickly*). A photograph ?

THORNTON. Yes—you may remember we asked you for one when first you reported Mrs. Martyn missing ?

CHRIS. I didn't give you one.

THORNTON. No—you said you hadn't got one.

CHRIS. I hadn't—my wife disliked being photographed.

THORNTON. Did she ?

CHRIS. Anything wrong with that ?

THORNTON. No.

CHRIS. What are you getting at, Inspector ? How could you publish a photograph ?

(*After a slight pause* THORNTON *speaks very quietly.*)

THORNTON. We had one by us, Mr. Martyn.

CHRIS. *You* had one ?

THORNTON. Yes.

CHRIS. I don't follow.

THORNTON. We thought it best to find out exactly how much you knew about the late Mrs. Martyn—and if you were ignorant, to warn you that she had been known to us—at one time.

CHRIS. *Known* to you ?

THORNTON. To the Police, yes.

(*There is a long pause.*)

CHRIS. I don't believe it !

THORNTON (*a humane man*). We realize it's difficult for you, Mr. Martyn—but we thought maybe it would be easiest if I came along and prepared you for the evidence that's coming from one or two witnesses at the inquest.

(CHRIS *looks stubborn, but says nothing.*)

THORNTON. As a matter of fact, I've brought one of them along with me now. I'd like you to have a talk with her, if you will.

CHRIS. You still believe the story of a pick-up in Maidstone on Thursday night, don't you ?

THORNTON. No—not necessarily. There is quite a possibility your wife never got to Maidstone at all.

CHRIS (*steadily*). Look, Inspector—I was married to Ruth for five years. No two people could have been closer or believed in one another more. Nothing you, or anyone else, is prepared to say about her now she's dead will shake my faith in her. (*His voice breaks slightly.*)

THORNTON. No, sir. (*He is slightly at a loss.*) Nevertheless, I'd still like you, and your mother, to see the lady I've brought along with me. She knew your wife well, and can give you the details better than I can.

(CHRIS *is unresponsive.*)

She will have to tell what she knows to the Coroner—it would be much better if you'd allow her to give it to you first.

CHRIS (*unwillingly*). Who is she ?

THORNTON. She'll explain that. Will you see her ? She won't keep you long.

CHRIS. Very well—but she'd better be careful, whoever she is !

THORNTON. Will you please ask your mother to come in here, and I'll go and fetch Miss Pearce.

CHRIS (*shouting*). Ruby Smith's not an unusual name. . . .

THORNTON. I'll fetch Miss Pearce—will you please get Mrs. Martyn ?

(*Without further ado, he disappears through the outer door.* CHRIS *walks up and down for a minute, repeating to himself* " Fantastic ! " *He then goes to the kitchen and shouts :*)

CHRIS. Mother—are you there ?

NAOMI (*off*). Yes—has the Inspector gone ?

CHRIS. Come here a minute, will you ?

(*There is a slight pause and then* NAOMI *comes through the kitchen door, still wearing her overall.*)

NAOMI. Well ?

CHRIS. Come in here.

NAOMI. What's the matter ?

CHRIS. The Inspector is saying the most outrageous things about Ruth.

NAOMI. What things ?

CHRIS. Some ridiculous story about her having been known to the Police at one time.

(NAOMI *stands stock still in the middle of the room.*)

NAOMI. Oh ?

CHRIS. I never heard anything so fantastic in my life !

NAOMI. What exactly did he say ?

CHRIS. Very little—just hinted at some mysterious " past "—he's gone to fetch a woman who he alleges knew her at one time.

NAOMI. Who is it ?

CHRIS. I don't know—but we'd better see her and squash this nonsense once and for all.

NAOMI. D'you want me to see her too ?

CHRIS. Yes—Thornton said you'd better be here.

NAOMI. Very well.

(*She takes off her overall, folds it and puts it on the dresser.*)

(*There are sounds of voices outside the door.*)

There they are now.

(*She moves to the outer door and opens it—The* INSPECTOR *and* MISS PEARCE *are standing outside.*)

Come in, won't you, Inspector ?

THORNTON. Thank you—I'm glad you are here. This is Miss Pearce—Mrs. Martyn.

(MISS PEARCE *is middle aged and capable looking. She speaks with a slight North Country accent.*)

NAOMI. Yes ? How do you do ?

MISS P. Ruby's mother-in-law ?

NAOMI. Yes. My son.

MISS P. I'm—glad to meet you both.

THORNTON. Miss Pearce knew young Mrs. Martyn well at one time. She arrived in Maidstone this morning to offer her help—so I want, if I may, to leave her to have a talk with you both. She can probably—clear up—one or two things for you.

NAOMI (*completely in the dark*). Yes ?

THORNTON. We shall want you at the inquest as well as your son, Mrs. Martyn, as you were the last person to see your daughter-in-law before she left here.

NAOMI. Yes—I understand.

THORNTON. I'll be waiting with the car at the end of the lane, Miss Pearce.

MISS P. All right—thanks, Inspector.

(THORNTON *looks from* CHRIS *to* NAOMI. *Wishing he didn't feel so sorry for them both, he makes good his escape without further ado. There is a slight pause after he goes.*)

NAOMI. Won't you sit down, Miss Pearce ?

MISS P. Thanks. . . .

CHRIS (*after another slight pause*). The Inspector says you knew my wife ?

MISS P. Yes. She—never mentioned me to you ?

CHRIS. Not as far as I remember. When did you know her ?

MISS P. She was a pupil of mine for some years.

CHRIS. Oh—you mean at the Orphanage ?

MISS P. She told you it was an Orphanage ?

CHRIS. That's what I understood—she said very little about it.

MISS P. I see.

NAOMI (*who has been regarding her curiously*). Would you mind telling us exactly who you are, Miss Pearce ?

MISS P. It seems I shall have to. I'm the Headmistress of an Approved School in Yorkshire.

CHRIS. An *approved* school ?

MISS P. That's right. At Westbridge.

CHRIS. But . . .

MISS P. Just what had poor Ruby told you about herself, Mr. Martyn ?

CHRIS (*repeating the tone he used to the Inspector*). All I wanted to know !

MISS P. Then you can hardly blame her if she didn't go into details about her past, can you ? (CHRIS *moves away slightly.*) Forgive me if I sound sharp, Mr. Martyn—but Ruby was one of my favourite pupils—and, I hoped, a real success story. All this has come as a terrible shock and disappointment to me.

NAOMI. Yes—we do understand, Miss Pearce. These last two

days have been very grim for my son too—and there seems there is still a lot more for us to learn.

Miss P. I travelled down from Westbridge through the night after I'd been on the 'phone to the Maidstone Police, and they'd told me they were not sure how much Mr. Martyn knew. I shall have to give evidence at the inquest in any case—but I thought maybe it would be—easier for him, if I had a talk with him first.

Naomi. That was very kind of you.

Miss P. Facts sound so harsh and uncompromising when they come out in public—I wanted to tell you something about the human side. I don't know what immediately led up to what happened on Thursday night—but I did know Ruby very well when things were at their worst for her, and I grew very fond of her.

Naomi. Why was she sent to you ?

Miss P. (*pausing, and glancing at* Chris). There were—a number of reasons. Mr. Martyn says she told him all he wanted to know. What *did* he want to know ? About her childhood ? Her background ?

Naomi. She was an orphan, wasn't she ?

Miss P. Well, naturally, not always. She wasn't a foundling, if that's what you mean. Did she tell you anything about her parents, Mr. Martyn ?

Chris. She said her mother'd been an invalid for several years.

Miss P. Did she tell you that she was one of three children ?

Chris. She didn't say three. She once mentioned something about a sister who died young.

Miss P. Did she tell you how that sister died—or about her brother ?

Chris. Her brother ?

Miss P. She didn't mention she had a brother ?

Chris. No.

Miss P. Ah—now I see where I'm getting to. I shall have to start at the beginning—and you must be patient with me, both of you. I've been working for the Home Office for twenty years, so if I seem to take a lot for granted that's shocking to you people who've led sheltered lives, you must forgive me.

Naomi. My son was in the Navy during the war—I hardly think his life has been very sheltered !

Miss P. No—possibly I'm using the wrong word. But I don't suppose either of you knows much about life in the London slums, and what it can do to children ?

NAOMI. Did my daughter-in-law live in the slums then ?

MISS P. Yes—in Camberwell. I believe her mother came from quite a good family, but she was always ailing, and quite incapable of coping with the drunken labourer she'd married, or her three children. Ruby seems to have been the only one with any sense. Both she and Dennis were frequently away from school, and in trouble with the Inspector—but it was chiefly because she was trying to look after them all. Dennis was a different case.

NAOMI. In what way ?

MISS P. He was rotten through and through, Mrs. Martyn—handsome and clever—but a born thug. Yet Ruby adored him. All the mistakes she made—all the trouble she brought on herself—Dennis was at the root of it all.

NAOMI. Please tell us everything.

MISS P. By the time he was ten he was mixed up with a gang of young hooligans in the neighbourhood—at twelve he was before a Juvenile Court. Later he was in Borstal—a deserter from the Army—and has done two prison sentences that I know of . . . (*She looks at* NAOMI'S *face.*) Am I going too fast for you ? I warned you we took these things for granted in my job. . . .

NAOMI. No—no. I was just thinking you *were* right to call my life sheltered !

MISS P. The youngest child, Elsie, died in somewhat dubious circumstances, when she was three.

NAOMI. In what way—dubious ?

MISS P. They decided to call it cruelty and neglect. The father was sentenced to a year's imprisonment.

CHRIS. God in heaven—have you much more to tell me about my wife's relations ?

MISS P. Don't you see that I'm trying to excuse your wife, Mr. Martyn ? Ruby wasn't a bad girl. She was the victim of terrible circumstances. That's why I'm telling you all this. I'm not trying to be sensational.

CHRIS. Go on. . . .

MISS P. While the father was doing his prison sentence, his wife died quite suddenly one night. Ruby was thirteen at the time. Terrified that they would be separated and put in different homes, she and Dennis ran away together. Dennis knew where to find a hideout, and their father was not interested in their disappearance when he returned from goal. They ran wild for nearly a year before the police caught up with them.

NAOMI. In what way—wild ?

MISS P. In every way, I'm afraid. They'd been harboured by a gang of crooks who found them useful. They were finally caught over a burglary. The gang escaped, and left the children to face the music. That was when they came before a Juvenile Court.

CHRIS. And what happened to them ?

MISS P. Dennis was sent to a home in Sussex. . . .

CHRIS. And my wife came to you ?

MISS P. (*slowly*). No, Mr. Martyn—not immediately. Ruby didn't come to me until six months later.

CHRIS. What happened to her then ? (MISS PEARCE *still hesitates.*) Come along—I've got to know everything !

MISS P. (*quietly*). Yes—I'm afraid you have. At the time they were taken in charge, it was discovered—that Ruby was going to have a child.

CHRIS (*with an intake of breath*). A child ?

MISS P. I'm afraid so, Mr. Martyn. She wasn't quite fifteen at the time. . . . .

(CHRIS *turns away again. This is the worst blow he has had to take, and he is speechless.*)

MISS P. I'm so dreadfully sorry, Mrs. Martyn. . . .

NAOMI (*hurriedly, because she's afraid* CHRIS *can't stand much more*). And—and you looked after her, Miss Pearce ?

MISS P. Oh no—not I—but she was looked after until her child was born. They sent her to me when she came out of hospital.

NAOMI. And she was with you for three years ?

MISS P. Yes. She was pretty hard-bitten when first she came. Hard and proud and, I'm sure, very ashamed of all that had happened to her. It was a long time before I could establish any contact with her—but she was always obedient, and worked hard. Mine is rather a special sort of school—the girls get a chance of better things than domestic work if they wish. Ruby had a secretarial training while she was there, and she learned quickly. She'd made her mistakes—but she paid for them with great courage. . . .

CHRIS (*swinging round suddenly*). Did it live ?

MISS P. (*taken aback*). Pardon ?

CHRIS. The child—did it live ?

MISS P. Oh—oh yes, I think so.

CHRIS. A boy or a girl ?

Miss P. I don't know—that part was all over by the time she came to me.

Chris. What happened to it?

Naomi. Chris, my dear, don't torture yourself. . . .

Chris. Well? D'you know?

Miss P. I'm afraid not, Mr. Martyn—that wasn't my department. I expect it was adopted—such children often are.

Chris. Did Ruth know where it was?

Miss P. No—I'm sure she didn't. It would be found a good home—these adoption societies are very strict, you know.

Chris. Why should I care?

Naomi. Chris—please. . . .

Chris (*in the grip of the green-eyed monster*). Who was the father?

Miss P. Ruby never told us.

Chris. Oh God—you mean . . .

Miss P. (*gently*). Look, Mr. Martyn—all this happened more than ten years ago—and Ruby has paid a terrible price for her sins—such as they were. When first she wrote and told me she was going to marry you, I advised her—so very strongly—to tell you everything. I never knew if she had—I don't know why she decided not to—but now she's dead. . . .

(Chris *is completely unresponsive.* Naomi *gives* Miss P. *an imploring look. She takes the hint, and rises.*)

Miss P. Yes—I think I'd better go. There is nothing more I can say. . . .

Naomi. Believe me, we are very grateful to you for coming, Miss Pearce. It can't have been easy.

Miss P. No—no it wasn't. Goodbye, Mrs. Martyn.

Naomi. Goodbye—and thank you.

Miss P. Goodbye, Mr. Martyn . . . (*But* Chris *is beyond speech. She takes a final look at him, and goes to the door.*)

Miss P. God bless you both. . . .

(*She lets herself out, closing the door quietly behind her. Her footsteps disappear, and finally a car is heard starting up and departing.* Naomi *looks at* Chris's *back for some time before she dares speak. When she does, it is with diffidence.*)

Naomi. Christopher? (*No answer.*) It was far better this way than hearing it for the first time at the inquest.

CHRIS. Yes.

NAOMI. Come and sit down, my dear.

CHRIS. I'm all right.

NAOMI. Please, Christopher—we've got to talk to one another.

CHRIS (*turning*). There's nothing to say.

NAOMI. Of course there is. Come along.

(CHRIS *shrugs slightly, but moves down and sits, prepared to listen— his face looks so dead, NAOMI pauses before her next move.*)

There are the children, Christopher.

CHRIS. Yes—all three of them !

NAOMI. I'm talking about Peter and Ba. However, you're feeling at the moment you've still got them and—you've still got me.

CHRIS (*looking at her for the first time*). I'm sorry, Mother— you and I don't seem to have made much contact lately.

NAOMI. We must try. The next few weeks are going to be grim—but if we face them together, we'll get through somehow.

(*Maybe it's her sympathy, but CHRIS breaks down. His face goes into his hands and he weeps. NAOMI rises and stands over him, but she has never been demonstrative and can't touch him even now. She just waits until the paroxysm passes.*)

CHRIS. Sorry, Mother—I'm a fool.

NAOMI (*awkwardly handing him her handkerchief*). Here !

CHRIS. Thanks. (*He uses it like a little boy and pulls himself together.*) If only she'd told me !

NAOMI. Would it have made any difference ?

CHRIS. I don't know—I just don't know. Why couldn't they leave me alone ?

NAOMI. They could hardly do that, could they ?

CHRIS (*wearily putting his hand to his forehead*). I can't believe it's happening to me. It's—it's as if one had to wake up.

NAOMI. I know. (*She waits for him to go on, not knowing how to help him.*)

CHRIS. I suppose you feel it's largely my own fault ?

NAOMI. How ?

CHRIS. You never trusted Ruth, did you ?

NAOMI. I didn't know her. I never felt she wanted me to know her—but I don't think " trust " is the right word. You trusted her yourself, didn't you ?

CHRIS. Yes—I was a fool!

NAOMI. You were happy for five years—I don't think you were such a fool.

CHRIS. Don't you? I think cuckold is the good old English word for what I've been!

NAOMI. No, Christopher.

CHRIS. She was with a man on Thursday night. Either here or in Maidstone, she was with a man.

NAOMI. We don't know that.

CHRIS. It was a man who—murdered her, wasn't it? She'd been mixed up with crooks in the past.

NAOMI. I think you're leaping to conclusions.

CHRIS. Of course I am—and so are the police. It's obvious Thornton thinks the man who killed her is mixed up with her past—otherwise why did he bring that woman along?

NAOMI. He brought her because she's going to give evidence at the inquest, and he didn't want you to learn all this in public. There's never been a suggestion that the murder is connected with Miss Pearce's story.

CHRIS. What other explanation could there be?

NAOMI. What about the robbery at Clifton Manor? They haven't arrested the man who did that—and I gather they were armed.

CHRIS. Ruth wasn't shot. (*He shudders.*)

NAOMI (*fearing he may go to pieces again*). Look—I don't know about you, but I could do with a cup of tea.

(CHRIS *makes no response.* NAOMI *gives him a long look, and then goes through the kitchen door. The rain begins to patter down again—*CHRIS *moves to the fire, and stands with his back to the room.* MISS MITCHUM-BROWNE, *under an umbrella, is seen outside the window. She peers in curiously, before moving to the door and tapping.* CHRIS *doesn't hear, so she taps again, and then opens the door softly, and peeps in.*)

MISS M-B. (*in a solicitous whisper*). It's only me, my dear boy! (*She lets her umbrella down, and shakes it.*) I'll leave my umbrella here. (*She props it up outside.*) I don't want to be a nuisance, or intrude (*but she comes in, and shuts the door*) but it seemed so unneighbourly not just to look in and tell you how *terribly* sorry we all are. . . .

CHRIS (*desperately*). Kind of you . . . !

Miss M-B. Not at all, my dear. *I* don't mind this weather—but it's so bad for you to be alone. You mustn't *brood*!

Chris. I'm not alone! (*He moves quickly to the kitchen door, and calls for help.*) Mother!

(Naomi *is back in the room like a shot.*)

Miss M-B. Oh, *you're* here, are you? I'm so glad, this poor boy shouldn't be left alone.

Naomi. He isn't!

Miss M-B. That's right. I only just looked in to offer my deepest sympathy—well the sympathy of the whole village, really. I'm not staying. (*But she is goggling with curiosity.*)

Naomi. Very kind of you. We're all right.

(*She moves up to the outer door, as if to see* Miss Mitchum-Browne *off the premises.*)

Miss M-B. Naturally I know you won't be wanting to see anyone—but I said to Mrs. Foster " They won't mind me—I'm such a very old friend. So I'll just slip along and tell them how much we are all thinking of them—I won't stay," I said.

(Chris *gives* Naomi *a helpless look.*)

Naomi. Will you thank them all, and say we appreciate their kind thoughts?

Miss M-B. I will indeed. (*She moves up a step or two—but she's not prepared to go yet.*) Er—the police haven't any clues yet, I suppose?

Naomi. No.

Miss M-B. Oh dear—I hoped they had. I saw a car drive off just now, it was the police, wasn't it?

Naomi. Yes—they came to make arrangements for the inquest.

Miss M-B. Oh I see. How awful for you—all the publicity, I mean! I suppose you *did* tell them what I told you the other night? About that dreadful looking man I saw with poor Ruth in the lane?

Naomi (*not without humour*). I thought you said it was Chris!

Miss M-B. Well I naturally thought at first—I mean I took it for granted. . . .

NAOMI (*finally*). Good morning, Miss Browne. Thank you for calling.

(MISS MITCHUM-BROWNE *has no alternative but to go, so she moves up to the outer door.*)

MISS M-B. Goodbye—so glad you're here to look after the dear boy—we'll be thinking of you !

(*She gets in a muddle with her umbrella.*)

(*She goes and* NAOMI *shuts the door firmly.*)

CHRIS. Oh God—I'd forgotten we'd that to face. They'll all know soon—and Christ, won't they gloat ?
NAOMI. We've enough to do without bothering about them ! I'm going to fetch that cup of tea.

(*She exits into the kitchen.* CHRIS *walks about the room, looking more and more desperate. The rain is coming down heavily again. He stands in the window, looking out at it.* NAOMI *comes back with the tea.*)

NAOMI. Come along—have some of this.

(CHRIS *comes down mechanically and she hands him a cup.*)

I've made it very sweet—I think it's a good idea.
CHRIS. Mother—after the inquest everybody's going to know Miss Pearce's story.
NAOMI. Yes—I'm afraid they are.
CHRIS. I don't think I can face it.
NAOMI. Of course you can—we'll face it together.
CHRIS. I'm sorry. . . .
NAOMI. Sorry ?
CHRIS. Dragging you into this.
NAOMI. It can hardly be considered your fault !
CHRIS. But it is. If I hadn't married a girl about whom I knew nothing. . . .
NAOMI. Look, Christopher. You married Ruth because you loved her. You did what you thought right at the time, and

you've been happy for more than five years. You must look at it all objectively. You've got the children . . .

CHRIS. Yes—God help them !

NAOMI. He will, my dear—they're so young, they need never know.

CHRIS. A pretty heritage they've got !

NAOMI. Environment counts more than heredity.

CHRIS. D'you believe that ?

NAOMI. Yes—I do.

CHRIS. I don't. Can environment make a negro's children white ?

NAOMI. That's different . . .

CHRIS. Is it ? Do you relish the thought of your grand-children being descended from jailbirds and Borstal inmates ?

NAOMI. They have quite a good inheritance on their father's side. . . .

CHRIS. But . . .

NAOMI. Look, Christopher—you've got to clear your mind of all this—or they'll never have a chance. We'll give them a happy life. . . .

CHRIS. Happy ? Here in Fellinge ?

NAOMI. It needn't be in Fellinge—we'll go away, and start all over again.

CHRIS. If the police will let us !

NAOMI. I don't mean at once. We've got to face all the publicity—there's no avoiding it. But it will die down. . . .

CHRIS. It'll last Miss Browne and the rest of them for the rest of their lives !

NAOMI. That's why I say we'll go away—we can live it down somewhere else.

(CHRIS *puts his cup on the mantelpiece, and begins to pace up and down.*)

CHRIS. Have you begun to think of what it's going to mean ?

NAOMI. Yes, Christopher.

CHRIS. Have you ? Police, detectives, newspaper men, photographers—all sticking their blasted noses in—this place will be a bloody peep-show. Charabanc loads of sightseers !

NAOMI. Christopher—please.

CHRIS (*working himself up and shouting against the rain*). God in heaven. The Martyns have stood for something here for centuries—and now we're going to be dragged through the mud. Headlines in all the Sunday rags—I'll probably be offered a fortune to write my story—"My life with Ruby Smith," by Christopher Martyn!

NAOMI. Stop it!

CHRIS. By God, I'll do it, too! How dare she do this to me—to all of us?

NAOMI. She's dead, Chris—whatever she's done, she's paid for it.

CHRIS. Yes! Slipped out of it all nicely, hasn't she?

NAOMI. You don't know what you're saying. . . .

CHRIS. A woman I loved! A woman I trusted! Blast her—for five years I've lived with someone I never knew! Thank God she is dead. . . .

(He is nearing hysteria—NAOMI moves to his side. As she does so, the latch clicks sharply, and the door opens slowly. RUTH staggers into the room—filthy, exhausted and dazed, but alive and unhurt. She leans against the lintel, and looks at them in a bewildered manner, as the rain lashes outside.)

RUTH. Chris—my darling—I. . . .

(NAOMI *and* CHRIS *swing round.*)

NAOMI. Ruth! *You!*

RUTH. Yes. I tried. . . . I couldn't. . . .

(Her voice trails away. She holds out her hand helplessly, and then sways forward, and falls into the room in a dead faint.)

CURTAIN.

ACT III

The following afternoon. (*Sunday.*)

(*The stage is empty when the curtain rises. The room is neat and tidy, as* NAOMI *has been in charge for two days.* CHRIS *passes the window, and comes through the door. He looks very tired. He takes off his hat and coat, and flings them on a chair, and slumps down in the arm chair by the fireplace.* NAOMI *comes down the stairs.*)

NAOMI. Oh hello—I didn't know you were back.

CHRIS. I've only just arrived.

NAOMI. You've been a long time. (*She picks up his hat and coat, and puts them on pegs behind the door.*)

CHRIS. I feel as though I'd been in the witness box for a couple of hours !

NAOMI. What was it all about ?

CHRIS. Going over everything again. After I'd 'phoned to say she was here, and they'd sent someone over to have a look at her last night, I'd imagined that would be the end of it so far as we were concerned, and we might be left in peace to clear up our own private cesspool. . . .

NAOMI. Chris !

CHRIS. But not at all—apparently it's a crime to identify a body wrongly—I've wasted precious time for them—God in heaven—the head was battered beyond recognition—the hair looked like Ruth, and there was the red mackintosh. . . .

NAOMI (*deliberately interrupting*). Have you had anything to eat ?

CHRIS. They gave me something at the police station. Did the doctor come ?

NAOMI. Yes—soon after you left.

CHRIS. Well—what did he say ?

NAOMI. He was pretty guarded—talked about a " psychic trauma "—whatever that may mean !

CHRIS. Good God—don't tell me old Foster's taken to trick cycling in his old age ! She's no more had a psychic whatsit than

I have—or a bloody blackout—she's just lying her head off. . . .

NAOMI. Christopher, we don't know—she's hardly said a thing yet. . . .

CHRIS. Is she up ?

NAOMI. Yes—I think she is. Dr. Foster said she was to be quiet for a day or two—but it's no good keeping her in bed against her will.

CHRIS. The police want to see her again anyway. Thornton's coming out.

NAOMI. When ?

CHRIS. Some time this afternoon.

NAOMI. D'you know what they want to see her about ?

CHRIS. Pretty obvious. They couldn't talk to her last night and they want to know where the devil she's been these last three days—and so do I.

NAOMI. Christopher—be gentle with her.

CHRIS. Why the hell should I ? She hasn't been very gentle with me !

(NAOMI *looks at him in some consternation. She has known him remote and difficult—but never hard and cynical like this.*)

NAOMI. If she has had a blackout. . . .

CHRIS. She hasn't !

NAOMI. But if she has—you mustn't badger her. The doctor said . . .

CHRIS. Do *you* think she has ?

NAOMI. I don't know. Her clothes were torn and muddy— she had a cut knee and a number of bruises—but no marks about the head to suggest concussion.

CHRIS. Have you talked to her ?

NAOMI. Very little—I didn't want to worry her.

CHRIS. What did she say ?

NAOMI. I took her up some food—but she couldn't eat it. She asked what had happened while she was away.

CHRIS. Did you tell her ?

NAOMI. I told her about the murder and your identifying the body wrongly.

CHRIS. Did you tell her about Miss Pearce's visit ?

NAOMI. I did not.

CHRIS. Why ?

NAOMI. My dear boy—I hardly felt that was my business— that's for you to tackle.

CHRIS (*grimly*). I'll tackle it all right ! Did she say anything else ?

NAOMI. No. I've kept out of her way.

CHRIS. Very wise !

NAOMI. Have they found out who the girl really was ?

CHRIS. No—that's the trouble—it's holding them up—damn their eyes.

NAOMI. It *is* still a murder case ?

CHRIS. Yes—and they still seem to think we're mixed up in it ! Pleasant, isn't it ?

NAOMI (*startled*). In what way ! How could we be ?

CHRIS. They think Ruth knows something.

NAOMI (*horrified*). Christopher, how could she ? They don't think . . .

CHRIS. She disappeared on Thursday night, didn't she ? This wretched girl was murdered on Thursday night—my—my immaculate wife has a police record—What d'you expect them to think ?

NAOMI. But they couldn't imagine . . .

CHRIS. They think she's shielding someone.

NAOMI. Perhaps she is. . . .

CHRIS (*filled with bitter, impotent jealousy*). Some bloody man out of her past—the father of her illegitimate child, perhaps !

NAOMI. Stop it, Christopher ! You're beside yourself.

CHRIS. Taking her part against me now, are you ? You haven't been so fond of her in the past !

(*He turns his back on her, and moves up to the window.*)

NAOMI. I'm not doing anything of the kind. But you've got to be just. Two days ago you were telling me you couldn't live without her. . . .

CHRIS. Two days ago ! The Ruth I thought I knew has gone. . . .

NAOMI. The son I thought *I* knew has gone !

CHRIS. Yes—he has ! He's come to his senses !

NAOMI. Or lost them. Christopher, doesn't it strike you that the man Ruth is shielding may be . . .

CHRIS (*seeing someone coming up the lane*). God—here's that blasted woman again—get rid of her before I go mad !

(*He rushes to the kitchen door, and disappears.*)

(NAOMI *stands still in the middle of the room.* MISS MITCHUM-
BROWNE *is seen passing the window. She carries a large bunch
of wilting Michaelmas daisies.*)

MISS M-B. (*popping her head round the outer door*). May I
come in—just for a second ?

NAOMI. Ruth can't see anyone, Miss Browne.

MISS M-B. Of course not. I'd be the last to bother her—I just
brought her a few flowers. (*She holds out the shabby bunch of
flowers and says sentimentally*) The last of my Michaelmas daisies
—I've stripped my little garden for her !

NAOMI. Very kind—thank you.

MISS M-B. Not at all—don't mention it ! (*In a hoarse whisper.*)
How is she ?

NAOMI. Dr. Foster says she is to be kept very quiet—

MISS M-B. Is she in bed ?

NAOMI (*hoping* RUTH *won't come in*). Yes.

MISS M-B. The poor dear. (*Eagerly.*) What happened ?

NAOMI. We haven't the least idea.

MISS M-B. Doesn't she remember *anything ?*

NAOMI. No.

MISS M-B. Oh dear, oh dear ! Chris must be terribly relieved
that she's back, isn't he ?

NAOMI. Naturally.

MISS M-B. Yes—of course. He's always trusted her so
implicitly, hasn't he ?

NAOMI. Why shouldn't he ?

MISS M-B. Oh—no reason at all. I'm sure she's made him a
wonderful wife !

NAOMI (*fixing* MISS MITCHUM-BROWNE *firmly with her eye*). You
were hinting at something on Thursday night, weren't you, Miss
Browne ?

MISS M-B. *Hinting* at something ? What an unpleasant
expression !

NAOMI. Yes—it is rather, isn't it ?

MISS M-B. Really, Mrs. Martyn—I don't know what you mean !

NAOMI. I think you do. You said Nurse Beeston had told
you something, didn't you ?

MISS M-B. But I refused to repeat it ! I said she was an
untrustworthy gossip. . . .

NAOMI. You were very anxious to repeat it—but I wouldn't
allow you to—I'll tell you what it was now.

Miss M-B. Please—I assure you . . .

Naomi. You needn't assure me anything—she'd told you Peter wasn't Ruth's first baby, hadn't she ?

Miss M-B. Really—I . . .

Naomi. Hadn't she ?

Miss M-B. Well—yes.

Naomi. Of course she had—the poisonous creature—She'd given me the same information.

Miss M-B. You ?

Naomi. Yes—I don't doubt she's passed it all round the village before she came to me—and I'm perfectly certain she didn't trouble to tell anyone my reply !

Miss M-B. Your reply !

Naomi. Yes ! I told her the truth—He wasn't a first baby. Ruth had had a miscarriage before she came to live in Fellinge—

Miss M-B. But I thought . . .

Naomi. Never mind what you thought. And another time don't be so anxious to believe an ignorant old village midwife, when she opens her mouth too wide ! When Ba was born they took my advice and engaged a proper nurse !

Miss M-B. Nurse Beeston has served this district faithfully for thirty years ! She had a perfect right . . .

Naomi. A moment ago you said she was an untrustworthy gossip ! She had no right to repeat her theories, and you had no right to believe them.

Miss M-B. I don't care to be spoken to in this way, Mrs. Martyn—Both poor Mother and I always kept ourselves to ourselves. This does happen to be my cottage, and I don't care to have it associated with unpleasant publicity—I have a right to . . .

Naomi. To turn the unsavoury Martyns into the street ? Well do so, Miss Browne. The Martyns have lived at the Grange for the last two centuries—you and your mother came here fifty years ago. . . .

Miss M-B. (*furiously*). We came here in 1913 !

Naomi. Oh—only forty years—well I feel we have priority— but if you wish us to leave this neighbourhood we are only too ready to do so ! I think, however, you'll find it a little difficult to remove us until the police have finished with an unpleasant murder case !

Miss M-B. The Police ?

Naomi. Yes ! Fellinge is very much in the news at present.

There was an armed robbery at Clifton Manor—a girl has been murdered in the district—my son identified a body wrongly— It's all going to add up to an unpleasant scandal. If you imagine my family and I are going to enjoy it, you are mistaken. The moment we can get away and start life afresh, we shall—but until that's possible, we'll be obliged if you and your friends will leave us alone and mind your own business !

Miss M-B. I have never been spoken to this way in my life— I think you will find that the Vicar and his congregation . . .

Naomi. I think both the Vicar *and* his congregation are going to get a surprise—Good afternoon.

Miss M-B. Good afternoon—

(She retreats through the outer door with what dignity she can muster. Naomi stands where she is, trembling with temper. Ruth comes downstairs. She looks ill, but is outwardly calm.)

Ruth. Oh—I—I thought I heard Chris.

Naomi. You did—he came back ten minutes ago. You should have stayed in bed.

Ruth. I'm all right. I want to see him.

Naomi. Very well—I'll go and find him. Would you like a hot drink ?

Ruth. No thank you.

Naomi. I'll get Chris.

(Naomi goes through the kitchen door. Ruth moves about restlessly. She sees two Sunday newspapers lying on the window seat, and picks them up. She scans the headlines of first one and then the other, her face concerned and strained. She hears someone moving in the kitchen and hurriedly replaces the newspapers. Chris comes through the kitchen door.)

Ruth (*moving to him swiftly*). Oh my darling—Naomi told me. What a terrible time you must have had. How awful of me to give you such a shock ! (*She puts her arms round him and leans her head against his chest. Chris stands immobile, with a grim face, but she can't see it.*) How good it is to be home !

(Chris deliberately removes her hands from his shoulders and puts her away from him.)

CHRIS. You'd better sit down.

RUTH. Yes—I still feel rather shaky.

(*She sits*—CHRIS *stands where he was. He waits for her to make the next move. She looks at him timidly, uncertain of his mood.*)

RUTH. It's good to be home, Chris.

CHRIS. Yes ?

RUTH. Home ! (*She looks round the room affectionately.*) It's so quiet without the children. When will they be back ?

CHRIS. They're well enough with Hannah.

RUTH. But I'm all right now, Chris, honestly. There's nothing the matter with me.

CHRIS. It takes a day or two to recover from a psychic trauma !

RUTH. A what ?

CHRIS. Dr. Foster's expression—not mine.

RUTH (*with a nervous laugh*). Oh how silly ! I just lost my memory.

CHRIS. Did you ?

RUTH (*too eagerly*). Of course—these last three days are just a blank.

CHRIS. How d'you know it's been three days ?

RUTH. Naomi told me.

CHRIS. I see. How did you find your way back ?

RUTH. I don't know. The homing instinct I suppose ! Something told me how to get back to you and the children.

CHRIS. Very clever, as you didn't know we existed !

(*She realizes she is on dangerous ground.*)

RUTH. Perhaps—perhaps it will all come back to me in time.

CHRIS. Perhaps it will ! What is the last thing you *do* remember ?

RUTH. I—I was going to the pictures with Sally, wasn't I ?

CHRIS. So I understood. Did you meet her ?

RUTH. Yes, I think so.

(CHRIS's *mouth tightens, which she notices.*)

I—I seem to remember talking to her.

CHRIS. Oh you do, do you ? Why didn't you come home with her ?

RUTH (*realizing she has made a mistake*). I don't know. (*She drops her face in her hands.*) Please, Chris, my head hurts—

(CHRIS *looks at her downbent head with contempt. He produces a packet of cigarettes and lights one for himself.*)

Can I have one, darling ?

(*He holds out the packet, and she takes one with a trembling hand. He lights it for her.*)

Thanks.

CHRIS. Do you remember getting on to the bus ?

RUTH. The bus ?

CHRIS. You went for the 6.40. Did you catch it ?

RUTH. Yes—yes I think I did.

CHRIS (*sharply*). Then you did get to Maidstone ?

RUTH (*desperately*). Yes ! I don't know !

CHRIS. And you met Sally outside the Granada ?

RUTH. I don't know ! Please, Chris—please ! You've no idea what it's like to lose your memory !

CHRIS. No—I've a very good memory—I remember way back. Do you ?

RUTH. What do you mean ?

CHRIS. Do you remember we've been married five years ?

RUTH. Why of course !

CHRIS. And how we first met ?

RUTH. Of course. (*She looks at him fearfully.*) What is all this, darling ?

CHRIS. I'm trying to find out how a " psychic trauma " affects one !

RUTH. Please stop using that silly phrase. Chris—it—it frightens me.

CHRIS. I'm being technical. I think you'll find the Police Inspector will be the same.

RUTH (*sharply*). The Police Inspector ?

CHRIS. A man called Thornton. We've seen quite a lot of him while you've been away—

RUTH. Oh—oh yes. About this—this murder you mean ?

CHRIS. Yes—about the murder—He's coming here this afternoon.

RUTH (*thoroughly frightened*). Coming here ?

CHRIS. So he said. He seems to think you can help them.

(RUTH *jumps up.*)

Sit down, Ruth !

RUTH (*sitting again, her hands clasped tightly*). How absurd—
How could I help them ?

CHRIS. I've no idea—He's coming to see you, anyway.

RUTH (*in a panic*). I can't see him ! I've nothing to tell him !
I—I can't remember anything !

CHRIS. Then you've only got to say so, haven't you ? What
is there to panic about ?

RUTH (*pulling herself together with a shaky laugh*). Sorry,
darling—I'm a bit nervy still !

CHRIS. So it would seem. When did your memory come
back ?

(RUTH *rises, she is trembling, but has otherwise got herself under
control. She moves to the fireplace, and throws her cigarette away.
She speaks slowly and deliberately.*)

RUTH. I remember waking up in bed, Naomi was beside me.

CHRIS. Just like that ? With no recollection of a thing after
you met Sally in Maidstone ?

RUTH. I'm not even sure that I did meet her.

CHRIS. No ?

RUTH (*after a slight pause*). Did—did this Inspector Thornton
find out anything ?

CHRIS. Oh yes—quite a lot. There were one or two other
witnesses as well !

RUTH (*clasping her hands more tightly*). Oh ?

CHRIS. Would you like me to tell you, or is your head still
hurting ?

RUTH. I'm all right. I'd better know.

CHRIS. Before you see Thornton ? Yes, perhaps you had !
There were conflicting stories. A policeman thought he saw you
talking to a man in Maidstone on Thursday night. You got into
a car with him, and drove off in the Ashford direction.

RUTH. He must have been mistaken !

CHRIS. Why ?

RUTH. Well—I mean . . . I—I don't know anyone with a
car.

CHRIS. But if you'd lost your memory you might have accepted
a lift from a stranger.

RUTH. Oh—yes !

CHRIS (*still watching her*). On the other hand, Miss Mitchum-

Browne insists she saw you walking down the lane with Ernie on Thursday night. . . .

RUTH (*too quickly*). I did ! I remember that !

CHRIS. And Ernie's certain he saw you talking to someone at the bus stop when the 6.40 went by.

(*She doesn't answer.*)

All most confusing, isn't it ?

RUTH (*in a whisper*). Yes.

CHRIS. But then you've always been mysterious, haven't you, Ruby ?

RUTH (*frightened*). What d'you mean ?

CHRIS. You said just now you remembered how we met ? Rather casual, wasn't it ?

RUTH (*with spirit*). You didn't seem to mind at the time !

CHRIS. You told me you were an orphan ?

RUTH. I was !

CHRIS. No family at all ?

RUTH. No !

CHRIS. Just a little waif and stray who'd been in an orphanage ?

RUTH (*beginning to panic*). Yes !

CHRIS. Where was it ?

RUTH. Where was what ?

CHRIS. The Orphanage ?

RUTH (*her panic increasing*). In London.

CHRIS. Which part of London ?

RUTH (*trapped and lying*). The south of London—Balham !

CHRIS. How old were you when you went there ?

RUTH. Quite little.

CHRIS. How old ?

RUTH. About—about ten, I think—

CHRIS. How long were you there ?

RUTH. Years—I don't remember.

CHRIS (*white with controlled anger*). Strange how your memory comes and goes ! Where have you been these last three days ?

RUTH. What has that got to do with it ?

CHRIS. I don't know—I'm asking you, Ruby Smith !

RUTH (*terrified*). Chris ! I don't know you ! What have I done to make you so angry ?

CHRIS. I'm asking you what you've done ! (*Breaking.*) You bloody little liar !

RUTH. Chris!

CHRIS. Lied to me from the beginning, haven't you? In an Orphanage were you? Go on—tell me some more. Tell me I'm the first man in your immaculate life!

RUTH. You're the only man I've loved.

CHRIS. Loved!

RUTH. Yes. I love you as I've never loved another human being. You're my life!

CHRIS. Your life built up of lies and cheating.

RUTH. I haven't cheated you!

CHRIS. Where have you been these last three days?

RUTH. I don't know—I don't remember!

CHRIS. You've been with a man!

RUTH. No!

CHRIS (*rushing at her and beginning to shake her*). I'll make you tell me the truth! You married me to cover your tracks, you harlot!

RUTH. No, Chris, no! I'll tell you . . .

CHRIS (*holding her in a murderous grip*). Never heard of a woman called Pearce, have you?

(RUTH *shrinks.*)

Ah—that jolts your precious memory! Does Westbridge ring another gong? That other bitch got murdered for living the life you've lived—and by God. . . .

RUTH (*limp in his grasp*). Why don't you kill me, Chris? D'you think I want to live?

(*He flings her from him—she falls on the floor, and lies inert. He looks at her for a second, horror in his face at what he has done, and why—then he turns on his heel and goes upstairs. RUTH lies where she is for a minute, her grief too deep for tears. Presently she drags herself up, and sits in a chair by the table. ERNIE appears at the window.*)

ERNIE (*looking at his lady rapturously*). Oi seen yer!

RUTH. Oh—Ernie. . . .

ERNIE. Oi can come in?

RUTH. Of course, Ernie—it's so good to see you!

(ERNIE *comes in through the door. He carries a small bunch of weeds.*)

ERNIE (*his love shining in his eyes*). Oi be glad.

RUTH. Glad to see me ?

ERNIE (*nodding*). Oi didn't tell *them* !

RUTH. Tell them what, Ernie ?

ERNIE. Oi said you was talkin'. You trust Oi.

Ruth. Of course I do—I always have, haven't I ?

ERNIE. You give Oi a list—Oi'll do yer shoppin' for yer !

RUTH. Not to-day, Ernie. It's Sunday ! (*Her tears come at last.*)

ERNIE (*registering carefully*). Sunday ! (*He looks at her timidly.*) Don't cry !

RUTH. It's silly of me. It's because I'm glad to see you.

(ERNIE *smiles down at her happily.* NAOMI *comes down the stairs.*)

NAOMI. What are you doing here, Ernie ?

ERNIE. Oi seen 'er.

RUTH (*faintly defiant*). He's glad to see me back—d'you mind ?

NAOMI. No, of course I don't.

(*For once in a way, she is uncertain of herself.* RUTH *takes command.*)

RUTH. Run along now, Ernie. You shall help me another time.

(ERNIE *carefully presents her with the bunch of weeds. He moves to the door, and then turns to* NAOMI.)

ERNIE (*defiantly*). She were *talkin'* !

(*He goes out, and disappears down the lane.* NAOMI *shuts the door after him. She stands looking at* RUTH, *who is fondling the little bunch of weeds, but says nothing.*)

RUTH. Naomi ?

NAOMI. Yes ?

RUTH. Chris has—found out about me while I've been away, hasn't he ?

NAOMI. Yes.

RUTH. And you know too ?

NAOMI. I know as much as he does.

RUTH. I see. (*Helplessly.*) What can I say to you ?

NAOMI. What d'you want to say to me ?

RUTH. I know you've never liked me, or trusted me. I can't ask you to forgive me for what I've done. But I have tried to be a good wife to Chris.

NAOMI (*cold but just*). You've been a very good wife to him—and a good Mother to Peter and Ba.

RUTH. *You* say that ?

NAOMI. Why shouldn't I ? You say I've never trusted you—have you ever trusted me ?

RUTH. No—I suppose not.

NAOMI. Why not ?

RUTH (*slowly*). Because I've always been afraid of you.

NAOMI. Afraid of me—or afraid of my finding out the truth ?

RUTH. Both, I think.

NAOMI. There has always been a wall between us, Ruth. I wish I had known what it was before.

RUTH. But surely. . . .

NAOMI. I've probably been unjust to you—but Christopher is my only child—his father died before he was born. Naturally I was anxious about his marriage.

RUTH. And you never thought me good enough ?

NAOMI. Did you resent that ?

RUTH. I suppose I did. Oh I know I had no right to.

NAOMI. You certainly didn't make things easy for me. You usurped Chris so completely—why, in the early days it was often three weeks at a time that neither of you came near me. Peter was five months on the way before I was told. . . .

RUTH. Do you know now that I'd had a baby before I was married ?

NAOMI (*calmly*). I knew at the time of Peter's birth. D'you imagine Nurse Beeston could hold her tongue ?

RUTH. Oh God—did she tell anyone else ?

NAOMI. I've had the pleasure of explaining to three people about an imaginary miscarriage of yours—with details !

RUTH (*looking at her in amazement*). You did that for me, Naomi ?

NAOMI. No. I did it for Christopher—and for myself.

RUTH (*looking away*). Yes. . . .

NAOMI. So I was more or less—prepared—for that part of the story. It came as the biggest shock of all to Christopher.

RUTH (*passionately*). I tried to tell him everything, Naomi—

I wanted to ! But he wouldn't let me. He said we'd both been unhappy, and now that he'd found me, he didn't want to talk about the past. How could I disillusion him ? I thought and thought until I felt I was going mad—and then it came to me that if I was making him happy—if I tried to *be* all he thought me —then I was—sort of—atoning for those dreadful years. I was a fool. He hates me now !

NAOMI. Does he ?

RUTH (*with a shudder*). You should have heard the things he said to me just now ! You should have seen the look in his eyes !

NAOMI. Can you blame him ? The whole bottom has fallen out of his life.

RUTH. I don't blame him—I blame myself—more bitterly than you know. I'll go away, Naomi. He can divorce me. I'll go now, without seeing him again if you like.

NAOMI. I don't like ! I think there is still a lot you have to explain to us both. You can't run away like that—it's cowardly. D'you know where Chris is now ?

RUTH. Where ?

NAOMI. On his bed—crying like a child !

RUTH. Oh my poor darling. . . .

NAOMI. I'm going to bring him down to you. Promise me you'll wait.

(RUTH *makes no reply.* NAOMI *gives her a final look, and goes upstairs.* RUTH *stays very still for a minute, and then panic seizes her. She snatches an old coat from behind the door, and runs outside. We see her pass the window, and then draw up suddenly, as the Voice of the Law is heard.*)

THORNTON (*off*). You're Mrs. Ruby Martyn, aren't you ?

RUTH. Yes. . .

THORNTON. Were you run . . . —were you going out ?

RUTH (*backing*). Yes—no—I. . . .

THORNTON (*coming into sight outside the window*). Could you spare me a few minutes ? It was you I came to see.

RUTH. Yes—sir.

(*She comes back into the room.* THORNTON *follows her in, and shuts the door.*)

THORNTON. Actually, I saw you last night—but you didn't

know. Let's sit down, shall we ? You still look tired. (*Ruth* sits.) I don't want to bother you more than need be. (*He sits beside her.*) But I think perhaps you can help us. . . .

RUTH (*too quickly*). I can't !

THORNTON. No ? This is a murder case—so the last three days are very important. Unfortunately your husband wasted valuable time for us by thinking the dead girl was you. . . .

RUTH. I wish it *had* been me ! I wish I *were* dead !

THORNTON. Not as bad as that, surely ?

RUTH. They've found out all about me. . . .

THORNTON. They had to know. It was coming out at the inquest. Miss Pearce was only trying to help.

RUTH. She's been here ?

THORNTON. Yes. She came as soon as she heard.

RUTH. Oh God !

THORNTON. It's been an unlucky break for you—it was a chance in a million the situation should have arisen.

RUTH. I was a fool ever to imagine I was free of the police !

THORNTON. Whether you are free or not depends entirely on yourself, and what you have to tell me about the last three days.

RUTH (*tough as* MISS PEARCE *knew her*). I've nothing to tell you ! I don't remember anything !

THORNTON. Why are you so afraid ?

RUTH. I'm not afraid ! I've nothing to tell you.

THORNTON (*trying a new approach*). Since we saw your husband this morning we've discovered who the victim really was.

RUTH (*on the alert*). Who ?

THORNTON. A member of the gang who broke into Clifton Manor last week. (RUTH *takes a sharp intake of breath.*) She'd been planted on the staff there about a month ago, and let two men into the house last Wednesday night. (RUTH *is trembling.*) Did you know there'd been a burglary ?

RUTH. NO ! (*A frightened pause.*) Did she—did she look like me then ?

THORNTON. About the same height, perhaps. But she'd apparently bought her coat at the same store as you. It was the coat your husband recognized—there was little else he could identify.

(RUTH *shudders—he changes the subject abruptly.*)

THORNTON. You have heard the conflicting stories of your whereabouts on Thursday night ?

RUTH. Yes.

THORNTON. You see how it complicates things for us ?

RUTH. Yes.

THORNTON. If you could straighten them out. . . .

RUTH (*hysterically*). I can't ! I can't ! I don't remember anything !

THORNTON. Come, Mrs. Martyn—d'you think you're being quite fair to yourself—or to your husband ?

RUTH. My husband ?

THORNTON. He's had a bad time these last few days. You love him, don't you ?

RUTH. More than anyone on earth !

THORNTON. More than your brother ?

RUTH. More than anyone ! (*She begins to cry—her defences are down.*)

THORNTON. You have been with your brother, haven't you ?

RUTH (*desperately*). Yes !

THORNTON. Ah ! (*He gets out a notebook, which he consults during the following conversation.*) When did you first see him ?

RUTH. I went down the field to close a pen—he was waiting there.

THORNTON. What time was that ?

RUTH. I'm not sure—somewhere round half past six.

THORNTON. What did he tell you ? (RUTH *hesitates.*) Well ? (*No reply.*) You *did* know about the job at Clifton Manor, didn't you ?

RUTH. Yes—he told me. He wanted me to hide him. I said I wouldn't have anything to do with him. I said I was through.

THORNTON. And then ?

RUTH. He asked for money. I told him I'd get him some if he met me in ten minutes time. . . .

THORNTON. Why ?

RUTH. *Why ?*

THORNTON. I thought you said you were through ?

RUTH. How can you be through with someone you've loved ? I'd got to help him.

THORNTON. Had he a gun ?

RUTH. Yes—but I didn't know that until later.

THORNTON. Well ?

RUTH. I collected four pounds, and he was waiting for me at the bus stop. Someone came down the road. . . .

THORNTON. Ernie Briggs ?

RUTH. He remembered ? I didn't think he would.

THORNTON. Ernie appears to have been a more reliable witness than we had imagined !

RUTH. Dennis pushed me into the hedge, and held me as if we were lovers. When Ernie had passed, he got out his gun, and told me he'd decided it was safest to take me on the run with him. The six-forty bus passed while we were talking.

THORNTON. I see—and then ?

RUTH. We walked for what seemed like hours—then Dennis saw a car outside a farm—it was unlocked.

THORNTON. He stole it ?

RUTH. Yes. He pushed me in. We drove all through the night. . . .

THORNTON. And he finally landed you in Liverpool ?

RUTH. How did you know ?

THORNTON. We arrested him on a merchant packet last night.

RUTH. Oh God ! What have you made me say ?

THORNTON (putting his notebook away). I was trying to find out if he'd really been with you from six thirty on Thursday night. (He pauses and looks at her.) You thought he might have committed the murder, didn't you ?

RUTH. Dennis didn't do it ?

THORNTON. The body we found had been dead at the most twelve hours. She couldn't have been killed before ten o'clock on Thursday night.

RUTH. Oh thank God—thank God. . . .

THORNTON. We still have to find the other member of the gang—the man the unfortunate girl met by appointment in Maidstone that night. We shall get him.

RUTH. And Dennis is in the clear ?

THORNTON. As regards murder—this time. But he's up for armed robbery again—and I hope, for your sake, he gets the longest stretch he's ever done. (He smiles at her suddenly.) You're a good sister, my dear—but stop letting that young blackguard ruin your life for you !

RUTH. My life's ruined, anyway.

THORNTON. Don't say that. Miss Pearce said you never lacked courage. Take a good bite on the blanket now. Is your husband in the house ?

RUTH. Yes, I think so.

THORNTON. Then straighten things up. Shall I call him in ?

RUTH. No! I've lied to him—he'll never forgive me.

THORNTON. He might—when he knows why you've been lying. I'll tell 'em if you like—but it would be better from you. (*He moves slightly towards stairs.*) Shall I?

RUTH. No don't! I'll tell them—I promise.

THORNTON. Very well. (*He pauses.*) Miss Pearce sent you a message, by the way.

RUTH. Yes?

THORNTON. She said " Give Ruby my love."

(RUTH'S *mouth trembles—she is near to tears again.* THORNTON *pats her shoulder.*)

THORNTON. Come—cheer up!

(NAOMI *comes down the stairs.*)

NAOMI. Oh—I didn't know you were here, Inspector.

THORNTON. I've just been having a talk with your daughter-in-law, Mrs. Martyn. We've cleared up one or two things.

NAOMI. Yes?

THORNTON. She wants to talk to you and her husband now.

NAOMI. He's just coming down.

THORNTON. Then I'll leave you—and I don't think I'll be bothering you again.

NAOMI. No?

THORNTON. Goodbye. (*To Ruth.*) Good luck!

(*He gives them both a final look, and goes.* NAOMI *closes the door after him.*)

NAOMI. Christopher is much calmer now, Ruth. I'll leave you alone with him.

RUTH. No—please stay, Naomi.

NAOMI. If you wish.

RUTH. I do—it will make it easier for Chris.

NAOMI. Very well.

(*She seats herself deliberately by the fire.* RUTH *moves about restlessly. There is another pause, and then* CHRIS *comes downstairs. His face expresses nothing. He stands, waiting for the women to make the first move—*RUTH *can say nothing.*)

NAOMI.   Ruth wishes me to stay, Christopher.

CHRIS.   Very well.

NAOMI.   Hadn't you better come in and sit down ?

CHRIS.   I'd rather stand.

NAOMI.   All right.   Go on, Ruth—you wanted to tell us some-thing.

RUTH.   I won't keep you long, Chris.   I promised the Inspector I'd tell you where I'd been.

CHRIS.   Yes ?

RUTH.   Please, darling—I want to tell you the truth.

CHRIS.   I'm listening.

(RUTH *looks helplessly at* NAOMI.)

NAOMI.   You've been with your brother, haven't you ?

RUTH.   Naomi !   You knew ?

NAOMI.   I guessed.   I tried to tell Christopher—

CHRIS.   When did you try to tell me ?

NAOMI.   This afternoon.   You weren't really listening.

RUTH.   I lied because I was certain Dennis was connected with the murder.   The Inspector says it was done while he was with me—so I can tell you anything you want to know.

NAOMI.   You were with him all the time ?

RUTH.   No—only until Friday morning—he took me to Liver-pool in a stolen car—I had no money—I was getting back for two days.

NAOMI.   How ?

RUTH.   Lorry hopping, mostly.   I walked a lot, as well.

NAOMI.   I see.

CHRIS.   Have you been communicating with your brother since you lived here ?

RUTH.   No—he found out where I was by chance.   He was one of the gang that broke into Clifton Manor.   The police got him last night.

CHRIS.   A pleasant brother-in-law—haven't I ?

RUTH.   He's not exactly a pleasant brother—But you can't stop trying to help people you've loved—even when they let you down.

CHRIS.   Can't you ?

RUTH.   I practically brought him up.   He was the only thing that mattered to me when we were little.   He was holding a gun when Ernie saw us on Thursday.   But he needn't have done.   I wouldn't bring him here—but I had to help him because of what had been.

CHRIS. Then Ernie did see you ?

RUTH. Yes. Dennis was holding me against him. Ernie thought we were lovers—but he didn't give me away.

NAOMI. No—he didn't. He's fond of you.

RUTH. We're kindred spirits, Ernie and I. He didn't know I was an outcast too—but it was a bond between us.

CHRIS. Supposing there hadn't been a murder—what then ?

RUTH. What then ?

CHRIS. What story were you preparing to tell ?

RUTH. I don't know. I was too tired to think. I just wanted to get back to my secret tent.

NAOMI. What's that ?

RUTH. " Keep me, oh God, in a secret tent, from the strife of tongues." It's a psalm we used to sing at Westbridge. That's how I've always thought of our life here.

CHRIS. Is that all it's meant to you ?

RUTH. No ! Not all. But you don't know how wonderful that part has been.

NAOMI. Yes he does—he told me so when you were missing. It's been a " secret tent " for him as well.

RUTH. Has it, Chris ? (*He doesn't reply.*) Chris, d'you remember when you first asked me, I said I couldn't marry you because you didn't know anything about me ?

CHRIS. Did you ?

RUTH. You know I did ! Have you forgotten what you looked like in those days ? So ill and nervy. D'you think it was easy for me not to tell you everything ?

CHRIS. You deliberately deceived me !

RUTH. No, Chris, no ! It was more awful than you can imagine. It would have been easier to tell you—and to lose you.

CHRIS. But you didn't risk it !

RUTH. No—I worked it out wrongly—like I've done so often. I wanted to look after you because I loved you. I made another sort of mess trying to look after Dennis. . . .

CHRIS. What about the other men ?

RUTH. There was only one other man—I'll tell you about him, if you like.

CHRIS. No !

NAOMI. Yes, Chris. I think Ruth should tell us.

RUTH. Thank you, Naomi. I know that's been the hardest

thing for you, Chris—the baby. You called me—a name—just now. You thought I'd been on the streets—didn't you ?

CHRIS. Miss Pearce said you couldn't name the father. . . .

NAOMI. No, Christopher, no. She said Ruth had never told them who he was.

RUTH. I didn't. He was dead by then, and in his way, he'd been kind to us.

CHRIS. Were you in love with him ?

RUTH. I was too young to know—I was all—sort of—mixed up. He was twice my age anyway.

CHRIS (*involuntarily*). Swine !

RUTH. Just weak, I guess. He never knew I was going to have a baby. He got killed in a street accident.

NAOMI. And you didn't tell the Authorities that ?

RUTH. Why should I ? I didn't care what they thought of me—I just hoped I'd die too when the baby was born.

(CHRIS'S *face has relaxed slightly, and he is now listening to the story.*)

NAOMI. What happened to it ?

RUTH. I don't know. I only heard his first cry—I never saw him. I hope he got with people who loved him and wanted him.

(*There is a pause.* NAOMI *looks at* CHRIS, *and sees his changed expression.*)

NAOMI. You didn't have a very happy childhood, did you ?

RUTH. I was fond of my mother—Her father was a parson—she ran away from home to marry Dad when she was seventeen—I was thirteen when she died.

NAOMI. You had a sister who died ?

RUTH. Yes—Dad hit her when she was crying—she died.

(CHRIS, *though silent, is watching her. There is no trace of self-pity in* RUTH'S *story.* NAOMI'S *voice is void of emotion as she questions her.*)

NAOMI. No—*not* a very happy childhood.

RUTH. It had its moments. I adored Dennis—he meant everything to me.

NAOMI. When did you realize what he was ?

RUTH. I don't know. He was a wrong 'un from the beginning I suppose. But you always makes excuses for people you love. Even when he came back last week I still had a shadow of the old feeling—It's a protective something—I dunno. I'm a fool.

(*She is conscious that* CHRIS *is silent through all this. She gives him a glance and is convinced he will never forgive her. She rises wearily.*)

So now you know everything. I'm not making excuses, or trying to justify myself. Miss Pearce told me to tell you—and I didn't. I wish I had—but there's nothing I can do for you but get out— and I will.

(CHRIS *says nothing.* NAOMI *looks from one to the other.*)

NAOMI. Where will you go ?
RUTH. I'll find somewhere.
NAOMI. Is that what you want, Chris ?

(CHRIS *gets up and moves to the window, his back toward them.*)

Is that what you want, Chris ?
CHRIS (*at last*). I don't know what I want !
NAOMI (*crisply*). Well I know what I want ! (*She rises.*) So you can both listen to me for a minute ! We've travelled a long way, this last week, the three of us, so I can be frank—I never liked you, Ruth, and I suspected you of many things—but I reluctantly had to own you made Christopher happier than I've ever known him. I've been jealous of you. I've been over-critical. But I now say to you, very humbly—don't go away, Ruth. We can none of us do without you.
CHRIS (*swinging round*). Mother !
NAOMI. Yes, Chris—that's how I feel. I'm not even convinced she should have told you about herself before she married you. As it is, she's given you five years of happiness—and but for this—accident—she'd have given you fifty more. It seems to me a perfect case of where ignorance is bliss . . .
RUTH. Oh Naomi—I've been so wrong about you !
NAOMI. Indeed you haven't ! I had absolutely no use for you at one time. I still didn't like you much when you disappeared into the blue three days ago. Now I'm merely exercising

my feminine privilege of changing my mind ! (*She moves to the kitchen door and turns.*) You'd better make up your mind what you want, Chris. The children will be back at any minute.

RUTH. The children ?

NAOMI. Had you forgotten them ? I told Hannah to bring them along for their afternoon walk !

(*Without looking at either of them, she marches through the door. RUTH stands where she is. The tears are running down her face, but she makes no sound. CHRIS turns from the window and looks at her. He is torn between humiliated pride and his old love for his wife. As he stands looking at her, PETER'S voice is heard in the distance, coming up the lane. RUTH hears it, and springs to life.*)

RUTH. That's Peter ! I can't see them, Chris—I daren't ! I know I'm no fit mother—I'll go away and leave them to you and Naomi—But don't let me see them—don't let me see them !

(*She stumbles blindly towards the kitchen door. The gay little voice comes nearer—CHRIS makes up his mind.*)

CHRIS. Ruth ! (*She stops at the door, her back towards him.*) Come here !

(*She turns slowly towards him. He holds out his arms. She goes to him in a flood of tears. He holds her head against his shoulder and strokes her hair as PETER'S voice is heard just outside. He knocks on the door and shouts "Let me in ! Where's my mummie ? " as*)

THE CURTAIN FALLS.

END OF PLAY.

Back cloth

Casement Window

Window seat

Front door

Arm chair

Open Fireplace

Dresser

Stairs and landing

Table and chairs

Kitchen door

FOOTLIGHTS

L

R

PROPERTY PLOT

Act I, Scene I.

On Stage. Toys, baby's bath, basket, clothes-horse and nappies, etc., scattered about the room.

Materials with which to make model ship on table—for Christopher.

Ruth's work box, containing needle, cotton, etc., and button.

Chris's evening jacket.

Sock with large hole from Ruth's work basket.

Mackintosh and hat from behind outer door for Chris.

Purse, containing money, in dresser drawer.

Money in an ornament on the mantelpiece.

Handbag and gloves on dresser for Ruth.

Off Stage. Red mackintosh—Ruth.

Handkerchief from bag—Naomi.

Skein of wool from bag—Naomi.

Matches from bag—Naomi.

Mug of milk—Ruth.

Knitting—Naomi.

Act I, Scene II.

On Stage. Empty pail, chicken food, cups and saucers about the place.

Cigarettes and matches.

Half a stale loaf on table.

Glass on sideboard.

Bottle of beer in sideboard.

Off Stage. Cigarette—Chris.

Sandwiches and brandy from basket—Naomi.

Notes and pencil, etc.—Thornton.

Act II.

On Stage. Duster—Naomi.

Packet of cigarettes and matches on mantelpiece.

Off Stage.   Sack—Ernie.
            Cigarette lighter—Thornton.
            Handkerchief—Naomi.
            Umbrella—Miss Mitchum-Browne.
            Tray of tea—Naomi.

Act III.

On Stage.   Two Sunday newspapers on window seat.
            Cigarettes and matches—Chris.
            Old coat from behind door—for Ruth.

Off Stage.   Hat and coat—Chris.
            Bunch of Michælmas daisies—Miss Mitchum-Browne.
            Small bunch of weeds—Ernie.
            Notebook—Thornton.